SWIPELOVE

*Navigating Dating Apps
to Build Quality Relationships
Beyond the Screen*

First Edition: September, 2019

Text Design: Andy Meaden meadencreative.com

Cover Design: Lewis Stone

ISBN 978-1-0904-5841-4

Dedicated to

Rich and Laure

who met each other
the old fashioned way

Contents

Introduction

You're stressed out.

From the dawn of time, selecting a mate has grown increasingly stressful.

It was easy for the first couples, the first neanderthals. There were only a handful of them to create the human race. We weren't populated all over the earth like now. Little to no competition. No freedom of choice. Just a group of beings who had to choose each other to keep the species alive. When someone is your only choice between life and death, they look much more appealing.

Then sometime after, while humans populated the whole planet, we invented marriage — a cross-cultural phenomenon, by the way. Our families arranged these marriages for us. This was good for the family because they could filter. They could pick someone for you they liked, who had a good family and stability (most likely financial). This was good for you too because you only had to choose between one to four mates, and your family already did the background check on them. It was an easy decision for you even if it wasn't strictly done for love and feelings.

By the 1800s in the United States, American families slowly loosened their grip on arranged marriages. Men started courting women on their own, taking the role of gentlemen callers. However, the practice of courting was controlled by women. According to Beth L. Bailey in her book *From Front Porch to Back Seat: Courtship in the Twentieth Century*, at public events, young women of mature age would give an invitation to men they had been properly introduced to. The young woman would provide a day and time she would be allowing callers to visit. (Women tended to have these same times set for each week.) When he had a time, he would walk over to a woman's house. At the front door, he would be greeted by the matriarch who would decide if he could be invited into the house parlor (a living room) to speak with her daughter. The family would give them this small bit of privacy but still be in earshot. The man and woman would talk for an hour or so, and then he would leave as other callers were scheduled for later. This was the 19th-century equivalent to a date.

But teenagers, mainly teenage girls, wanted more control. And rightly so. The roaring 1920s brought us jazz, radio, and affordable cars – but more importantly for this book, it brought us our modern understanding of **dating**. Beth L. Bailey further details that dating was a practice that evolved because growing urban living didn't offer a lot of private space in one's home, but instead offered the public space of the city and the appeal of no parental supervision. Through widespread magazines of the time, the practice of dating reached the country, replacing the gentlemen callers altogether (from front porches to back seats). Like courting, the practice of dating was controlled by women. Women in bars would encourage suitors to pay for their drinks and pay for their outings in exchange for a chance to have a "date" scheduled with them. Since the 1920s America was experiencing the industrial and economic boom, men proved their value by paying for dates. Women proved their value by the amount of dates they had – demonstrating their popularity and the demand for their time. The exchange came with many advantages. Women could continue being sexual selectors without spending money. Men could spend money to prove their worth to a woman. And with the advent of the affordable automobile, even teenagers could get out of the house to gain privacy and gain freedom to explore romantic relationships where they wished.

Now, families no longer hold the power over selecting a partner. Dating gives us the ultimate control over romantic selection.

WE GET THE FREEDOM TO CHOOSE NOW.

But we also have to be responsible for finding a good partner. One who is honorable, financially stable, compatible with you, hopefully compatible with family and friends; one who is responsible for themselves, civil, attractive, etc. We have to do all the filtering on our own.

Worse, we have to trust that we alone are good at filtering. That this person we are going out with is not manipulating us. We have the final say on whether this person stays. This is a heavy decision.

Our date is also doing the same work. Our date has their own laundry list of qualities they're looking for, which means we too have to be financially sound. We need to have a good job. We need to be compatible with them and their family.

But worst of all, WE HAVE TO ADVERTISE NOW!

We have to grab the attention of a mate. We have to be walking billboards, advertising that we're worth talking to, worth dating, worth getting married to, worth having sex with, worth having children with. We have to be *on* all the time. And not amongst three or four or 10 people, but potentially 1000s of people we come in contact throughout our day.

Everyone is advertising themselves. There's mass competition. But who really is going to pay attention to you when there's this many people jumping around for attention? People get discouraged from decision fatigue.

What do I say? When do I say it? How should I say it? Is what I'm wearing okay? Should I not approach this person? Should I stop waiting? Should I just go for it already?

You're probably stressed after reading all this. And that's the point. Stress from dating is at an all time high. We don't like to talk about it, but we know we're stressed.

But those days are over.

When we better our relationships, we better our communities, our companies, and ultimately our country!

In all I do, I believe in laughing at myself so that we all know we're allowed to make mistakes and grow free of stress.

I'm still laughing at myself for how stressed I was about dating before.

Now I believe in a world where we can all relax when we go on a first date. Where we, of course, are smitten with curiosity and possibilities of a blooming relationship, but **feel no anxiety about failure**.

Through this book, I'll show you exactly what you can do to enjoy your own dating life, become a better person, and how I went on genuine, classic, gentlemanly dates with lovely, well-mannered, noble women.

But you have to be willing to make mistakes.

Principle 1: Laugh at yourself.

By laughing at yourself you are willing to admit your mistakes and learn from them. You are allowed to relax during failure. Recognize that you aren't *all that*, but you also have value in just being you. After all, the search for a mate is the search for a partner to grow with, so if you are already *done* growing, you don't need a life mate.

Don't take yourself too seriously. Be willing to grow and change and try a new approach. Be malleable. Be humble. Laugh at yourself.

This is a small part of what SwipeLove is about. I look forward to inviting you in and serving you with all I know. Soon you will learn how to build relationships beyond the screen.

PART 1

BEFORE YOU DOWNLOAD A DATING APP

Chapter 1:
How to Approach Dating

Years back, my friend Tana met a boy. I asked her what she wanted in a relationship. She answered, "I just want to date and see where things go." Three weeks and a few dates later, she gave me an update on the boy:

He asked her to be his girlfriend.

But she was frustrated. She didn't want this. I asked her what she wanted. She reminded me that she just wanted to see where things would go. I said, "Well this is where things *went*." The boy was being clear with what he wanted. But he was unsuccessful. It wasn't necessarily his fault either. Tana didn't know what she wanted, so he was doomed from the start. They remained disappointed for a few weeks because of wasted time and energy.

The 2-Question Approach

Before we dive into understanding how to meet someone, you need to answer two questions for yourself. On the next page, you will write out your answers to the following questions to determine your *direction* and *destination*.

1. What is the reason you want to date?
2. Based on your answer, what does your end goal look like?

It doesn't matter to me what your answers are to these questions, but it matters to you. What does matter to me is that you answer these questions for yourself. You need to know why you want to do this odd tradition of spending ample time with a stranger until suddenly they're not a stranger anymore. You need to allow yourself some direction; you need to draw yourself a map so you know where you're going.

1. For what reason do you want to date? Circle one or more of the answers below:

- Intimacy and sex?

- To find love?

- Stave off loneliness?

- Marriage? Committing to another person?

- Meet new people?

- Go to new places?

- Other?

2. Based on that answer, what does your end goal look like? Make sure it's measurable. Consider these questions when your begin writing on the next page.

Intimacy and sex?

o What level of intimacy do you want? What level of
intimacy is too far? How often do you want to have
sex? How long should sex take? Explorative sex? Same
partners? For how long?

To find love?

o Is love a steady boy/girlfriend? Is love seeing each
other every day/week? Is love living together? How
much vulnerability do you show in love?

Stave off loneliness?

o Is loneliness cured by one date a week? Three dates a
month? Ongoing dates with the same person? How
long do these dates need to be? Two hours?

Marriage? Committing to another person?

o Does committing mean supporting this person's life?
Sacrificing your own priorities at times? What are
you willing to sacrifice? What should your partner be
willing to sacrifice? How long will you go out before
committing? How much do you need to know about
this person before you can confidently commit? Who
does this person need to be?

Meet new people?

o How many people do you want to meet? What kind
of people do you want to meet? People who challenge
you? People like you? People who are different?
People who can teach you something?

Go to new places?

o What kind of places do you want to explore? How
many places? How far way from your home do you

want to explore? What are good places for two people to see together?

Get out a sheet of paper and answer these questions. There is space provided below. The more specific your answer, the sharper your aim will be. You can't know where you're going until you pick a destination. You can't reach that destination until you pick the direction you wish to head. Writing out a mental picture of what you want at this basic level will save a lot of energy and pain in the long run for both you and any date you meet. A person you date deserves this courtesy from you as much as you deserve it from them.

What is the reason you want to date? Based on your answer, what does your end goal look like?

_____

_____

_____

_____

_____

_____

_____

_____

_____

_____

_____

The Four Phases of Dating

Why are you even going on a date?

You already know your direction – e.g.: sex, get married, etc. – but why do we date at all? What's the end goal of dating?

There's four basic phases in dating that I think we can all agree on:

Phase 1: Going out on dates with any number of people.

Phase 2: Commitment to a person to be your boyfriend/girlfriend.

Phase 3: Commitment to be engaged to that same person.

Phase 4: Commitment to marriage with that same person.

Basically, you're dating because you want one of these four levels of commitment and the benefits they allow. The end goal of dating is to get to Phase 4 and to remain in Phase 4. This is what dating was originally designed for, and the structure does this well. But this is not how a lot of people use the dating structure – many people travel up and down the phases to their heart's content or discontent. Depending on why they personally choose to date, they may never even hit all the stages. It's up to you.

Understanding Phase 1

I'm here to help you with the on-boarding process. In this book, I'm only focused on Phase 1, and how to get to Phase 2, because most people try to get at least that far. Once you're headed towards Phase 2, you don't need me. I certainly don't want to become a third person in your relationship.

What's the goal of Phase 1?

The goal of Phase 1 is to keep going on dates with people until you find someone you want to commit longer.

That's it.

There should be no pressure in this stage. It's a phase to "sniff each other out." See how much the other person matters to you on a surface level. See how much crap they're trying to sell you. A first date, a second date, or a third date with someone does not mean commitment. (However, the more dates you go on, the more you imply a higher level of commitment.) You should remember that any pressure you feel at this phase has only been added by you or someone you know and is completely unnecessary.

Remember that with dating apps, a first date will feel more like a blind date. You barely know anything about this person, so you won't feel too committed on this first date. The pressure to have a good date is lessened because you're meeting a person who has little to no ties to your community of friends or family.

A lot of us growing up in the 21st century have garnered a different definition of dating than the previous century. We tend to see the Phase 1 dating process as some sort of immediate commitment. A first date is seen as a big deal. From a certain angle, it certainly can be. May be this is why we avoid the word "date."

But the real commitment starts at Phase 2. If you can end the relationship over text, it's not a big commitment.

Pep Talk #1:
Why I Wrote This Book

In June 2017, I was frustrated and bored. I was between jobs in Los Angeles, so I had time on my hands. I had some money saved, but I was cooped up in my apartment.

I hadn't spent time on my love life since I moved to LA a year before. I wanted to discover what dating was like in LA. I had tried using Tinder my first year, but I could barely get one date using it. I was worried. I wasn't interested in the hook-up culture, the Hollywood romance, or the club scene. I wanted a woman who was more down-to-earth and wanted a long-term relationship, and I thought my chances were slim for finding someone like this in LA.

One day at home, I went on the Google Play Store and realized I had never had success on dating apps. I figured *I* had the problem with Tinder before, and I needed to find the perfect dating app for me. The perfect app would be fun to use, keep giving me matches, and actually give me in-person dates. (What a concept.)

So I downloaded all the dating apps on the Google Play Store I could find — Tinder, Bumble, OkCupid, CoffeeMeetsBagel, whatever came up.

I uploaded a set of photos onto each app and wrote a description for each of my profiles. And I left them on my phone. I decided to pop on to them whenever I felt like it, and when I found the perfect app, I would get rid of all the others. But after a few days of doing just that, I discovered I wasn't looking for the perfect app, but the perfect apps!

I was getting significantly more matches and conversations with having all these apps on my phone than if I kept just one.

In the early weeks and with some pre-date planning, I was able to go on four dates a week! None of these women were that stereotypical Hollywood type I was trying to avoid. They were down-to-earth, humble, beautiful, and worth more than one date.

I realized I had stumbled on a new mindset for dating. I wasn't concerned with fate having the final say in my life. I had control over my dating life in ways I had never experienced. More importantly, using multiple dating apps paired with my strategies could work for anyone no matter their race, sex, sexual preference, or orientation.

This is when I knew I had to write this book.

Look, I was frustrated. You're frustrated. Maybe you don't have a good track record with dating apps. Maybe you live in a small town where everyone knows you, and that makes it harder to date. Maybe you've moved to a new town, and you have no clue how to start meeting people.

I needed to share this with folks like you who are looking for love. Too many people are sitting at home without a date because they feel they don't have any other options. I was there. This book has you in mind.

I promise if you follow the strategies I present in this book and do what is required (which isn't much), you will have more dates than you know what to do with. You'll be in a better position to choose the life you wish.

This book grants you permission to change your life.

Chapter 2:
Why Have Dating Apps Anyway?

I can maintain four quality dates per week using dating apps. I have never met and learned about so many new people so quickly in my entire life. It can be overwhelming. I don't recommend this pace for most people – even myself. But this pace is possible.

Ever since we started dating independent of our families, we've felt proud about the level of control we have in relationships. But we admit we have no control when we say things like:

"It will happen when it's suppose to happen."

"You'll find someone when you stop looking."

"Someone will come when you least expect it."

These phrases reveal how much we surrender control to fate. We surrender to inevitable waiting.

If you can meet four new people in one week, you no longer have to pointlessly wait to find a new person. Even one date a week kills the waiting. You regain some control. Sure, most dates statistically will be failed relationships. But you can fail faster now. You can learn what you like and don't like in relationships with more precision. You can control the pace of your dating life with dating apps. Four dates per week. One date per week. Two dates per month. It's up to you now.

But don't put technology on a pedestal.

Principle 2: Humans before technology.

Humans were not made for technology.

You know this.

Technology was made for humans, so humans could use it. But there is a problem. Some phone technology is made to manipulate humans. Among other things, this tech addicts you so you keep using it.

We can sit in front of our TVs all night. We can scroll endlessly on our phones. Folks always want to play one more game of Candy Crush...waiting for food in a restaurant...with their children across the table. Humans were not made for their attention to be sucked away by technology.

But what are humans made for? Certainly for their children I hope! Humans are made to give attention to other humans. Often. Our brains are wired for this.

We do this unintentionally already. We speak with our friends. We spend time with those we call family. We call assistants to book appointments. We sometimes smile at strangers on the street when we make eye contact. We interact with humans every day. When we are with other humans, we have a sense of belonging.

We have tech like dating apps that allows us to meet more humans. We should remember why we use dating apps. Dating apps are tools. A way to fix a problem or make your life easier. Nothing less.

A hammer makes it easier to put nails in a wall as part of a bigger project. This makes sense. Using a hammer to put nails in a wall for no reason is watered. Having a hammer with no intent to use it is just weird.

Dating apps make it easier to meet more humans. Nothing less.

Using dating apps to only compare yourself to others is demeaning.

Using dating apps to only receive compliments is watered down.

At the end of the day, you want to be meeting people for dates. Anything short of this is not the intended use. Choose to meet people before spending time on dating apps. The only reason you spend time on the app is to keep meeting people.

Humans before technology.

Why Use Dating Apps?

Meeting new people in-person has become *less frequent* as the 21st century continues. Up through high school, socializing comes frequently. You see the same kids every day. You rotate classes six to 10 times a day. If you don't like anyone in one class, you only have to wait 50 minutes before you can move on to a new social environment. You also have a lunch period somewhere in the middle purely to meet new people and talk. You can see the same person at least five times a week and due to repeated schedules you can likely make a close friend in two weeks. This is good for dating because the rate at which you can gather friends increases the rate at which they can put you in front of potential dates.

In college, meeting people becomes a bit trickier. Certainly, you still have a school campus filled with thousands of students, but no one has the same fixed weekly schedule. Each day is different. Everyone gets lunch at different times. Students aren't all released at 3:00pm to enjoy the rest of the day to hang out. Because schedules gets so much messier, you have to be intentional about meeting up with each other and getting to know each other. Even if you're intentional with setting up lunches, dinners, and coffee runs, your friend may not be. The whole relationship can become unbalanced because you feel like you're the one doing all the work. This puts a strain on your friendship. If you haven't developed those skills by college, you'll have some catching up to do. Unfortunately, most college students don't like to commit to plans, so most of the population will struggle getting together routinely. Additionally, the struggle of commitment affects going on dates just the same.

Your friend network will likely shrink, decreasing your chances of recommendations for potential dates.

Once you're launched into the adult world working full-time, your friend network shrinks even smaller because college friends move away. Or you may have even moved somewhere new and have to build new friends from scratch. Or if you came back home after college, you'll see that the friends you had are gone or have changed. Again, your social environment has changed. The point is you no longer have a network of thousands of students where you share notes on people to meet, places to go, events to see, and date ideas to try.

During this time, a shrinking friend network can be an unreliable resource for finding dates.

Thankfully, there are tools called dating apps that can put you in front of people. People who are seeking a date as much as you are. Without the need of a community group, you can start meeting people on your schedule. As the community around us shrinks, dating apps become a new avenue for meeting people.

The 3 Speed Bumps of Dating Apps

Dating apps require a different mindset than traditional dating. The problem is most people don't use dating apps correctly. People hit a lot of speed bumps that slow them down. Dating apps work if you have a solution for these speed bumps. The common speed bumps people face are as follows:

Speed Bump 1: You don't match with people frequently, so it takes a long time before you can chat with someone.

Speed Bump 2: When you do match, you can chat, but people are often hesitant to respond, so you can't talk.

Speed Bump 3: If you do talk with someone, setting up a first date can be hard because of the fear of rejection and schedule availability.

Ultimately, materializing a date is still difficult even though a dating app can put you in front of a bunch of potential mates and show you a trove of people. Anyone with the goal of "get a date" will run into all three of these speed bumps and get decision fatigue from questions like:

- What should I do to get more matches? Do people not like me? Should I change my profile?

- When should I chat with this match? How long should I wait? What should I say? How should I say hello? How long should we talk before it gets annoying?

- Should I ask this person on a date? Should I tell them it's a date? How should I ask so that I don't get rejected? How should I ask so that I am being clear with them? Should I ask them today or tomorrow?

We've all asked these questions. This is decision fatigue. We become exhausted. There's too many questions. We can answer a few of them, but after awhile we run out of energy to keep up. We lose momentum.

But don't worry. I've developed some systems to smooth out all the decision-making. What do I mean by 'systems'? In Scott Adams' book *How to Fail at Almost Everything and Still Win Big*, Scott explains,

> "A **system** is something you do on a regular basis that increases your odds of happiness over time […] The requirement of a system is that a reasonable person expects it to work more often than not. Unlike goals,

systems have no deadlines, and on any given day you probably can't tell if they're moving you in the right direction."

A system saves you time and energy in making decisions. Plus, you save more time and energy the longer you go. This is because you build patterns on which decisions to make and when. Suddenly dating apps will be second-nature. You'll wonder why you questioned dating apps in the beginning. You'll become more competent. More self-aware. More efficient as a person. You'll gain speed. And with speed comes...momentum.

Pep Talk #2: You're Not Desperate. You're Resourceful.

Would you rather twist a screw into a wall by hand or with a screwdriver? Or what if you had a drill in your toolbox? You would use the most effective resource available to you. You wouldn't hold on to your pride and twist in a screw by hand simply because any other option may make you look incapable.

We shame ourselves into not using dating apps. Dating apps are tools. They are neutral. The more tools you have in your toolbox, the more options you have to create the result you want. Dating apps don't mean you are incapable, and they don't mean you want a shallow relationship. Dating apps are whatever you make of them. These tools are available to us to increase our chances of meeting great people.

Most of us have a few social media apps on our phones — Facebook, Twitter, Snapchat, Instagram, Tumblr are five of the most common. Even if you don't use them every day, you still have them on your phone, right? Why? Because you'll eventually want to get in touch with someone or see what's new.

It's the same thing with dating apps, yet we don't download a handful.

All these dating apps are free. You can shut off any unwanted notifications. So why did you stop at one or two? Does it make you look desperate? Hide your dating apps in a folder if need be.

To your friends, you may appear desperate. But they haven't helped you meet someone in awhile, right? You know what you're doing. You are resourceful.

At the end of the day, don't let your concerns with appearance stop you from being fulfilled with your relationships. Download some dating apps and see if it works for you. Watch your number of quality dates increase.

Chapter 3:
Why Do I Need Momentum?

Imagine you are riding a bicycle.

As you pedal, the bike moves and builds momentum. You don't focus on pedaling. Or the bike chain. Or switching gears. You focus on what's ahead. You focus on moving the bike forward. Once a bike has established momentum, it will continue on its own — it doesn't just stop the moment you stop pedaling.

You can do the same with dating apps after you set up your profiles.

In an ideal world, you will start swiping profiles. Once you make a match, you can immediately chat with a person. You can then ask them out on a date. Now you have a date.

But don't stop the bike — don't stop swiping profiles or chatting or asking people on dates. You keep putting in the effort to keep the momentum going. Keep pedaling.

Principle #3: Keep building momentum.

If you keep the momentum for a week, suddenly you may have 10 matches, five of whom you are chatting with, and two you scheduled for dates. That's just the start. You will only gain momentum as you continue.

Now, remember this is the ideal picture. Will you match with everyone you swipe on? No. Will every match want to chat with you? Not likely. Will every person you chat with agree to a date in-person? No.

But you're not focused on whether one person says *yes* or *no* — this is the heart of building momentum. Focusing on the *yes* or *no* is decision fatigue. This is important. This is the number one thing slowing you down. Giving too much attention to one person you barely know. This stops momentum.

Pace yourself. Don't focus on each decision you have to make. Focus on the overall momentum you are building up.

Also, it's a waste of time. Keep your focus on building momentum knowing you ultimately will get matches and go on dates. The more time you put in, the more people you will meet.

This is the mindset. Zoom out and focus on the big picture of the dates you will have in the coming months. Don't focus on the one person who may have not responded today.

One last thing. Think of one dating app as a single-speed bike while 10 apps is a 10-speed bike. In the same way you would switch between different gears to keep momentum and maintain pacing, you will switch between apps to do the same.

The more gears you have, the less effort you will need to exert when you go up and down hills. The more dating apps you have, the less effort you will need to put in when setting up in-person dates. The more time you will have back to focus on the rest of your life while the apps work in the background.

Like pedaling a bike, it doesn't feel like you're doing a lot. You just swipe a few profiles and call it a day. Or send a hello to a new match. It may not feel like much, but it is the little pedals that move the big wheel and keep momentum going. With a little effort the whole bike speeds forward.

With dating apps, momentum is that feeling you get when dates are falling into place, and you have many chats going on in multiple phases of development, and you don't have to worry about whether one person responded to your most recent chat, or whether you had great chemistry on your last date because you know that you have lots of things going on, and you are moving in the right direction, you are using a good system, and good things will inevitably come out of this.

But if you are starting from a standstill, how do you build up that feeling of momentum? By pedaling.

With dating apps, pedaling is all the small actions that you do on your apps, in text messages, and on dates. Pedaling means even if you already have a date lined up that evening, you still swipe a few more profiles before you call it a day. You still start a conversation with a new match. This is pedaling. It may not feel like much, but a little pedaling moves the bike and keeps momentum going.

Killing momentum means you shut the entire machine down every time you get a new date. You hang up the bike. This is an exhausting way to date because the most work in online dating goes into getting the "bike" up to speed. However, once you have built momentum, the whole bike continues forward with ease.

Keep building momentum.

More on Systems vs. Goals

Building momentum is a systems mindset. Instead of seeing each individual date as a task, imagine those tasks contribute to a big machine that produces constant output. One machine requires less emotional willpower than one goal.

Scott Adams further explained the difference between having a goal and having a system:

> *"A goal is a specific objective that you either achieve or don't sometime in the future. A system is something you do on a regular basis that increases your odds of happiness in the long run.*
>
> *...The system-versus-goals model can be applied to most human endeavors. In the world of dieting, losing twenty pounds is a goal, but eating right is a system.*
>
> *...If you achieve your goal, you*

*celebrate and feel terrific, but only
until you realize you just lost the thing
that gave you purpose and direction.*

*...With goals, people are fighting
discouragement at each turn. With
systems, people are feeling good
every time they apply their system."*

I used a system to write this book. The system was "write for 20 minutes every day on the train." A goal would have been "write a book." I know eventually a larger body of work will come from writing 20 minutes every day. Now, you have a book in your hands.

For our purposes, another example of a goal-versus-system is:

Goal – I'm going to get a date.

System – I'm going to keep dating *regularly.*

Regularly can mean once a week, once every two weeks, twice a week — whatever works for you. But choose a specific amount. You'll want to put yourself in a systems mindset as we continue in our dating endeavor. Don't worry. It will be simple.

Pep Talk #3: Dating is a Numbers Game

Some people say dating is not a numbers game.

Some folks say, "Going on dates doesn't increase your odds of finding a spouse."

Not going on dates doesn't increase your odds either. But more importantly, you don't sharpen dating manners. You don't learn how to be a good date or how to identify someone being a good date towards you.

Some folks say, "If you go on enough dates with enough people after enough time, you're bound to find a great person you connect with and can build a beautiful relationship with."

Not exactly. But you're bound to learn how to have quality dates and identify someone who's marriage material.

In this way, you're odds do increase. Just not in the way you expect.

One added condition:

You have to be willing to settle for someone who isn't perfect. Why? That is the only kind of person out there.

So settle for that.

Take control of your life. Go on dates. Become a better a date. Increase your odds.

There is a group of people depending on the narrative of fate, and it's not working for them. This book is for them. This book allows you to control the pace of your dating life. A date once a month. Once a week. Twice a week. Whatever you want.

Dating is a Numbers Game. You have genuine, fair control.

PART 2

HOW TO USE APPS TO BUILD DATING MOMENTUM

Chapter 4:
The First System for Dating Apps

I had a simple goal my first week using a dating app – go on a date. But I talked to no one that first week. Or second week. Or third week. I only chatted with one person in my first month. I knew I wasn't excited about this person after chatting for a moment. But 30 days of no date made me restless. I wanted to meet *somebody*. We met up for coffee. We never met up again. I achieved my goal after a month. I felt like I wasted my time and energy. I got my hopes up over one month. All I could do was take the one opportunity the one app offered. I needed a system for dating apps. So will you.

Your first system starts like this:

Don't use only one dating app at a time.

I tried that. Using one dating app limits your chances of ever meeting someone. And if you do end up meeting with someone for a first date, you tend to put pressure on yourself to make sure that date works out because your chances are limited. After all, if it fails, this was the only date you had all month. It may be a while until the next one.

Selecting Apps

Instead of using one app until I get frustrated, I use multiple dating apps simultaneously because it solves a few major problems:

1. **You garner more attention**. With five dating apps, your face and profile are in front of easily five times as many people than if you used only one app. This already takes care of Speed Bump 1.

2. **You get to sort through more people**, but you will find different kinds of people on each app. You may find your "type" more on one app than another app.

3. **You can't be restricted by the design of one app's algorithm** because you have multiple apps balancing out your options. One app may not show you the kind of people you like.

4. **You nullify any app's weaknesses, and take advantage of each app's strengths** because you are leaning on many apps. Not just one. (More on this in a moment.)

5. **You increase your chance of chatting and getting in-person dates**, therefore you have no need to put pressure on yourself due to scarcity of dates. Keep building momentum.

Basically, using multiple apps allows you to date on your terms with increased odds instead of being limited to the restricted rules of one app. You'll come to find that even using a highly populated app like Tinder is still, on its own, quite limiting in how it allows you to meet people.

Your objective for this next activity is this:

Have five to eight dating apps set up with profiles on your phone by the end of the week.

If this sounds like a lot of work, skip to Pep Talk #4 right now. I want you to understand now that this will not be a lot of work.

So here's what you do:

1. **Start by downloading nine to eleven dating apps** from your app store. This sounds like a high number, but it will do you good. You'll delete some later.

I have placed a brief index of dating apps in the back of this book to help you. Here's also a list of dating apps to download in no particular order:

Tinder	Bumble	Coffee Meets Bagel	OkCupid
Hinge	Facebook	Clover	Happn
Once	ChristianMingle	Crosspaths	Hot or Not
Plenty of Fish	Badoo	Zoosk	Grindr
Jaumo	BeWild	Blendr	MeetMe

2. **One by one, set up a basic profile** for each app. (I will tell you how to set up better profiles soon.) Again if this seems like a lot of work, skip to Pep Talk #4 right now.

3. **Explore each app.** You'll find that some apps allow you to

chat with people quickly. Some show you fewer profiles, but they give you profiles of people you're immediately willing to talk to. Some have fun concepts. Some are downright annoying to use.

4. **Keep all of the apps on your phone for seven days.** Even if you immediately hate one app, continue to fiddle with each one when you have a moment. You may find some grow on you.

5. **After a week, feel free to start deleting apps.** Don't go below five even if you're not using them. Again, the objective is to have at least five apps you can utilize to build momentum for setting up dates.

6. **After deleting, take another look around the app store.** There are dating apps you may have missed on your first go. I found OkCupid this way, and it became one of my favorites.

7. **If you want some more information on dating apps**, there is an appendix in the back of this book briefly describing the strengths and weaknesses for many of the current dating apps.

After a week, you should have five to eight apps, five to eight bike gears, you can use to keep gaining momentum and maintain a pace for your dating life.

My Personal App Preferences

The apps I have on my phone are:

1. Coffee Meets Bagel
2. Bumble

3. Hinge

4. OkCupid

5. Tinder

6. The Inner Circle

What did you find out after fiddling with these apps for a few hours?

When I did this, the first thing I realized was Tinder makes it really hard to get dates if you want to save time. Tinder requires you to sort through profiles *one by one,* like someone's profile, wait for that person to sort through their own assembly line of profiles *one by one (that's sooo tedious),* hope… I'll say it again, *HOPE* they like your profile, and then FINALLY, you can chat. Maybe. If they respond.

What I have noticed is most people who have tried dating apps have only used Tinder. One app cemented their opinion. I'm not here to talk crap about Tinder. But I am here to shake up your mindset about what else is out there and what you can do about your dating life.

If all you're using is Tinder, you're dating life is going to be slow. Period.

Did I keep Tinder on my phone? Yes, supplemented by other apps.

You may have found that Bumble is basically another Tinder, but it limits your profile word count more. This could make it hard to get attention if you don't know what to write. How are you supposed to find something in common with a person if you can only tell him/her three things about yourself?

Maybe you noticed Facebook will recommend you events to check out for you and your matches. This makes thinking of date locations potentially easier. (But don't worry, we cover date ideas in a later section.)

Or maybe you noticed that Hinge requires you to like a specific photo or description in a person's profile if you want to connect with them. This is good for finding more intentional matches.

Perhaps you discovered that OkCupid allows you to send a message to someone even if you haven't matched with each other's profiles yet. First, that's a HUGE time saver. Second, chatting gets a person's attention faster than your profile alone. OkCupid may not have as many profiles, but it gives you a lot of freedom with the profiles you do see. Maybe you like this. I find it helpful.

Again, if downloading a few apps seems like a lot of work, skip to Pep Talk #4 right now.

Otherwise, congratulations! You've taken your first step into a larger world. You're already choosing to learn new things! If you've downloaded some of those apps, you're learning what works for you, and what designs and tools you have at your disposal. You're choosing to think differently than you have before, which is crazy hard to do.

You are setting your foundation for going on more dates in the coming months. You're taking control of your dating life. This is a brave action to take. You may not be sure what you're doing, but you trust you are moving in the right direction. You're getting ready to gain momentum.

Pep Talk #4:
Sacrifice 720 hours?
Or Just One Hour?

I've inevitably heard some push back from sharing my ideas.

Asking someone to use five dating apps instead of one app can easily be interpreted as a chore or as homework. As something you have to keep up with rather than enjoy.

Honestly, my cause is for everyone to feel stress-free in their dating life, so I recommend this method because it is easier. I think there are too many of us out there who are not fulfilled with dating, courting, and love because we are stressed.

I understand the kind of loneliness and frustration many have about dating and relationships. I've been there as most of us have. So I'm sharing what helped me turn frustration into enjoyable times and good memories. I choose to not take myself too seriously.

Using one app will continually frustrate you. No matter how much time you decide to put into it. One whole month can go by without even a meeting for a drink. That's 720 hours with no results.

You could have at least four dates in that time. One date a week.

I'm asking you to give yourself just one hour. You're certainly worth an hour of your own time to set yourself up for fulfillment.

Honestly it can even take nine minutes to be realistic.

Take two minutes and go through your phone, your Instagram, and your Facebook and download or screenshot the photos you like of yourself. You'll use these on all dating apps.

Take another three minutes and write a quaint description of yourself and what you want. You'll use this on all dating apps with maybe some revision.

Take another two minutes and download all the dating apps you can find.

And take another two minutes with each app to plug in your photos and description.

That's it.

From there… go on those apps when you want.

For 10 minutes today? Great. For 30 seconds? Again, great. Only use one app this week? Cool, you like that one. Only swiped through three profiles tonight? Great, you're hopeful.

Not at all this week? Great, you can see if anyone reaches out.

Just being out there and going at your own pace will bring so many more people who you are actually interested in, and will certainly bring you people who want to know who you are, where you're going, and if you two click.

That's 720 hours of frustration, and nine minutes to change it.

Chapter 5:
The Photo System

Do you remember Speed Bump 1 when using dating apps?

Speed Bump 1: You don't match with people frequently, so it takes a long time before you can chat with someone.

Through setting up your profile, you will learn how to attract more people to you and match more frequently while being authentic at the same time. This will shorten the wait time you usually have to deal with before you chat with someone. Now that you've seen what kind of dating apps are out there, let's focus on your profile. We'll start with photos and then move to profile description in the following chapter.

Which Photos Do You Use?

How are you perceived on dating apps? What are your photos showing about you?

Don't try to impress anyone. You should laugh at yourself for that. That's serving yourself. Rather *impress upon* someone who you are. This is serving others.

Principle #4: Serve your date. Not yourself.

Most people, often in good nature, want to craft their best image on dating profiles. Perhaps even better than who they actually are. This does a few good things – you come off as attractive, you have more confidence on the given app, and you can emphasize your favorite traits.

But this causes you to miss out on one of the most appealing qualities – *authenticity*. Sure, you want someone to see how deep you are by presenting a photo where you're sitting on a cliff meditating. But how often are you on a cliff meditating? Maybe you want to show off five photos of your body in nice underwear, but how often do people regularly see you in your underwear? It may not be how you normally present yourself.

You want to serve somebody? Be yourself. One of the most attractive qualities people attest to is someone confident with who they truly are. Someone willing to be vulnerable. So share tiny bits of authenticity from the outset in your photos and also in your description.

Four Steps to Emphasize Authenticity in Your Photos

1. **Choose to show four to seven photos.** Not a peek, not your life story. Just a glimpse. (I like to present five total photos, but this is up to you.)

2. **For your first two photos, find candid photos of yourself.** One with a genuine smirk or laugh does great. The second photo can be another candid laugh. Overall just make sure you're not posing for the camera

in the photo. This sets a truthful tone from the moment someone sees your profile.

- Make sure ONLY YOU are in these first two photos. If other people are in these first two photos, it's difficult to distinguish whose profile this is. And now people are already comparing how attractive you are to others. If you're the only person in the photo, no comparison can be made.

- (Side note: When your first photo shows multiple people, a lot of swipers go by this rule: "The ugliest person in the photo is whose profile this is.")

- When I say candid, that basically means NO SELFIES. Selfies are posed. Don't kid yourself.

Figure 1: A good candid photo like this sparks more curiosity than a posed photo.

3. **For your third photo**, this one can be more posed, but consider your personality. Of course you smile, but are you also sassy or sarcastic? Show a photo where you're rolling your eyes. Are you dramatic? Showcase that big personality. Are you a klutz? Show yourself losing your

balance somewhere. This can be very endearing, and again you're standing out from the crowd because people don't show those kind of photos.

- **Pro Tip:** Avoid showing off how cool you are in this third photo. First, you're not as cool as you think you are. Second, dating profiles are FILLED with people trying to show off how cool they are. More often, you gather how pretentious a person is from those photos more than how cool they are. Third, people think you're cool because you are authentic. You are cool because you genuinely are dramatic or a klutz or calm. If you posed against a brick wall with sunglasses and a nice jacket, your coolness is a facade.

Figure 2: Our dork side is always more endearing.

4. **With your final photos, showcase activities you've done.** Have you scaled a mountain? Do you run marathons? Do you perform on stage? Plop those great photos in to fill out the end. Those photos are also often candid. These photos are talking points that potential matches will ask you about later.

- Give a variety. Don't show three photos of the same activity. Are you a one-trick pony? Of course not.

Seven Things to Avoid with Your Photos

Now, let's talk about some things that aren't ever helpful:

1. **At all cost, avoid selfies.** They're often pixelated and have poor lighting. Even though everyone takes selfies, a selfie can also portray you as vain. Furthermore, the more selfies you upload, the fewer friends people think you have because one begins to ask, "Why did no one else take a photo of him/her?" If the photo is distorted, don't add it. Even if you really like the photo, if it's blurry, out of focus, too pixelated, etc., leave it behind. A bad photo tells potential matches you don't have any better photos to show. While if they never see a bad photo, they don't think you have any.
   - If you don't have better photos, take some during your day. Tell your friends you need some photos for a profile. More than likely, your friends will get more creative ideas than you would on your own. It can be a fun day out.

Figure 3: Unless Jeff Goldblum is in your distorted selfie, don't upload it.

3. **Don't hide your face.** Don't show only half of your face, don't show only one eye in the corner of the frame. I notice girls do this more often. It's just a waste of a photo. We want to see your face. And when you hide it, we intuit a lack of confidence in yourself.

4. **Don't use photos with the Snapchat dog face filter or anything similar.** Again, girls seem to use this more than guys, and I have no idea what the appeal is. Sure it softens your face, but... you have a dog nose on your face. I've never known a person who swiped right on a profile because they saw a dog face photo and said, "Oh that's the person I want to date." (The only exception for using this filter is if you make some obvious ironic joke like also having a doggy dish in front of you... That's kind of funny and thinking outside of the box... I'm still not sure it's worth it.)

5. **Do not connect your Instagram.** Many dating apps allow you to connect your Instagram to your profile. Don't do it. A potential match can form the wrong opinion from one photo shown out of context. It's generally better for them to see your social media once you've met in-person and built a connection.

6. **Don't show only one or two photos.** This gives the sense that you're hiding something.

7. **Don't use graduation photos.** This final point is my own pet peeve. Graduation photos are only self-congratulatory. I'm happy you graduated, but you likely have student debt and still don't know what the next step is in your life.

That's a lot to consider, but most of these points I expect are easily understood.

Remember: Don't be self-serving. Don't impress, but rather *impress upon* someone who you are. When you're swiping through other people's profiles, what impression do they make on you? What photos make you swipe *yes*? What photos turn you away? What profiles make you feel shut out? Do you feel like they're putting their photos out there for you? Or are their photos on display for them?

Serve your date. Not yourself.

Pep Talk #5:
The Yin and Yang of Technology

We are intimidated by technology. We don't know how it works. Is anyone sure how Google's algorithm works? We also can't navigate technology 100%. Only a handful of people are making money through the internet. Only a handful of people are currently finding love through dating apps.

But we see technology as positive, which it is. However, we're relying heavily on technology for our social connections even though we don't know how it works. We may in fact be using it wrong. This heavy reliance may make us unbalanced.

We've created a duality between humans and technology. Where before technology was for utility, and humans were for connection, we have started leaning towards humans for utility, and technology for connection. How many Facebook friends do you have? How many trusted friends do you have for certain?

You may have seen this image before.

The yin and yang symbol. While I'm no expert in Daoism, the yin and yang illustrates my point. The yin and yang from Daoism illustrates the duality in life. For our purposes, the yin and yang are briefly explained in this excerpt from the Tao Te Ching's second passage. (This English translation is by Ursula K. Le Guin.)

*Everybody on earth knowing
that beauty is beautiful
makes ugliness.*

*Everybody knowing
that goodness is good
makes wickedness.*

*For being and nonbeing
arise together;
hard and easy
complete each other;
long and short
shape each other;
high and low
depend on each other;
note and voice
make the music together;
before and after
follow each other.*

Focus on the black and white dots in the yin and yang. The dots depict this — there's a little good in the bad, and a little bad in the good. There is a little chaos in order, and a little order in chaos. There's a balance.

This is why I appreciate dating apps, actually. As a technology, the end goal of dating apps is for you to stop using the dating app once you have found a partner. Dating apps are not designed to be used forever. They are the true social media. What we call social media is designed for never-ending use which keeps you less social.

Even with dating apps we can get carried away. We can get addicted to endless swiping if we don't know what we're doing. So we need a principle in mind to hold us steady. The principle is "humans before technology." You are using dating apps to find a person. This maintains the healthy, balanced dynamic with the technology. You'll know you are unbalanced with dating apps if you become so connected to the technology that you prefer it to humans. Give this a second thought.

If you are concerned about overusing dating apps or other apps, there are plenty of app blockers you can download onto your phone. You can set times to discipline when you use your phone and create a healthy relationship with technology. I personally use the apps AntiSocial and Block on my phone for free.

Technology is designed to serve us. Humans are designed to serve each other.

Humans before technology.

Chapter 6: The Invitation System

You've got some spectacular photos for your profile. Sweet. But you still have a description to write. I'd rather frame it as an invitation. What do you write for this? Can you write too little? Can you write too much?

Principle #5: Be constantly inviting

Ultimately, you're trying to invite someone on a date. But before a date, you invite someone to have a conversation with you. Before a conversation, you invite someone to look at your profile and swipe.

People go on these dating apps to meet new people. People who demonstrate they want us to be in their lives (at least for one date) are ultra-appealing. It's a reciprocal thing. When we already know someone wants us around on this basic level, we are more comfortable to be inviting towards them.

Something most people do with their profiles is list a bunch of adjectives about themselves. You've probably seen lists like:

I am adventurous, fun, easy going, artistic, and extroverted.

OR

I like coffee, a person with a sense of humor, trying new things, and The Office.

There are two problems with this kind of listing.

First problem: these are vague qualities and interests that make anyone say, "No duh, we all like someone with a sense of humor." And "Gee, I would hope you're easy going." They don't paint a picture of who you are as a person. They're just empty adjectives. But we'll solve that problem in a moment.

Instead of saying a vague word like "adventurous," tell me how you're adventurous:

My roommate and I always look for a new path every time we hike on the weekends.

OR

I've been to 26 states, France, England, Australia, and New Zealand. I am still looking to hit up Italy and New York City.

These above descriptions tell me not only that the person is adventurous, but if they view adventurous as a local exploration or travel to far off places. Goals are also listed like "finding a new hiking spot" or "Italy is next on my list to see." People learn much more about who you are from being a little more specific. Show don't tell.

Second problem: lists are **not inviting**. Your potential match will have nothing to talk to you about. These are simply standard lists. They tell me basic qualities, but don't show anything about one's actual personality. They're just dry and boring. They're certainly not inviting because you're putting it on your match to make a conversation happen later. When someone is talking to you in the chat, it can honestly feel like forcing a question to ask, "So you said you're adventurous. Where have you been recently?" That's mildly awkward for someone to ask. You could have simply said where you have traveled. Give us topics worth asking you.

Be inviting. Serve your date. Not yourself.

Making Your Description into a Fun Game

One way to be inviting is to be playful. Make a game out of your lists. Try one of these:

- Two Truths & A Lie
- Strengths & Weaknesses
- My Ratings

The First Game: Two Truths & A Lie

List two truthful facts about yourself and one false fact. But be specific like this:

- I only wear Nike shoes.
- I've been to 26 states and think Kansas is completely underrated.
- I'd rather receive daisies than roses.

Figure 4: My description on the dating app Bumble

This game is great because you've given your match a built-in question. "Is _____ the lie?" From there, you can let the conversation flow. But more so, your match is learning a lot about you.

Based on the earlier description, this person likes Nike shoes, so they are tied to certain brands, and they're a casual dresser. They're obviously someone who likes to travel and seems to have a soft spot for podunk towns even though they may not live in one. Finally, they prefer daisies meaning they're not big on classic traditions but still enjoy getting flowers (and gifts in general). The choice of daisies can easily imply a friendlier person rather than a more romantic person who wants roses.

Now, sure, some of this is being implied, but it's building an image of a real person, not just a list. Certainly one of these is a lie, but once the conversation begins, you'll find out what that is. In this case, you'll find out what states, shoes, or flowers they actually like.

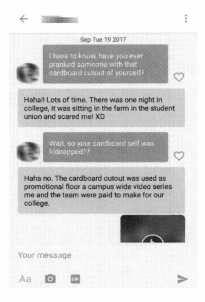

Figure 5: A woman initiated our conversation based on Two Truths & a Lie on Bumble

The Second Game: Strengths & Weaknesses

List things you have a lot of experience with or knowledge on as strengths. Then, list things that you like so much they make you "weak" as weaknesses. Make sure to be specific. Like so:

Strengths: Star Wars, good first impressions, American Civil War History, getting lost in Belgium, puns

Weaknesses: Tina Fey, my sister's corgi puppy, people who send Thank You cards, cracker-crust pizza

This game helps you stand out from the crowd a bit. It just doesn't tell someone what you're like, but it conveys what you're good at it. And rather than saying just what you like, it lists great ways to get on your good side. It's more creative than just saying what you are.

Strengths: This person is knowledgeable about Star Wars so they could be a big sci-fi fan. They explicitly say you can expect a good first impression from them which takes a certain level of confidence to even say. They're probably into history if they like the American Civil War, and they most likely have a funny story about getting lost traveling around Europe.

Weaknesses: A good thing to immediately note: this person likes cracker-crust pizza, which might be a good idea for a restaurant date. Maybe even a way to encourage them to join you for a first date. They also revere gratitude in people and probably have read Tina Fey's biography. If you're a dog person, this is a bonus.

The Third Game: My Ratings

List good qualities under the humorous guise of fake reviews from fake dates.

My Ratings

5 Stars: "Great date for weddings. Good dancer." – Miss California

5 Stars: "Took me on the sunset hike of the century." — Bumble Date

5 Stars: "He's my phone's background." – Mom
5 Stars: "Intelligent." – Sherlock Holmes

1 Star: "Stop asking me for a rating, you weirdo." – Anonymous Date

This ratings game is powerful for two main reasons.

1. **You can BRAG about yourself** without sounding like a jerk because you're hardcore flirting.

2. **You can swing around your sense of humor** and get people laughing because of your self-deprecation.

Based on this description, this person claims be a good date for weddings, which doesn't only involve dancing. They claim to also make good impressions in front of family members. They also claim to know at least one great hiking route and heavily imply their romantic chops. The rest of this shows off their humor, but there's plenty to flirt and ask them about after this point.

With these three games I've provided, it is wise to not use only one game and then leave your description alone. Use these games as a way to supplement your description or even use two games to fill out your description.

Make Your Description Authentic

I set up four quality first dates in one week because of this method. You likely wouldn't know where to begin if I told you to be authentic. But *writing down* your authenticity is even harder. How do you explain the deep, consistent truth about you?

A profile description which offers the truth about you is alluring. People can sense the truth. The truth is magnetic. The truth attracts people seeking it. (Truthseekers are always a good group to date.) The truth also repels those who deceive. (This is a group you should avoid.) You want to build trust early? Offer the deep truth. There's nothing more inviting.

What do you value? Why are you... *you?*

"People don't buy *what* you do. People buy *why* you do it." These are the words of Simon Sinek, one of my favorite advisors on authenticity and the author of *Start With Why.* (Well worth the read.)

Another way to say his quote is: People don't buy the qualities in your description list, but why those qualities are on your list. It's a different way to think, isn't it?

Why do you do what you do? If you want to allure people who have the same values, you'll want to have the answer. Note: This description is separate from any games I mentioned earlier.

How To Write an Authentic Description

1. **Answer the question "Why do you do what you do?"**
   This requires a few days of thinking. But it's essential to painting an authentic, alluring picture of yourself.

   Try this exercise:

   Think back through your past. What jobs did you like? What classes were you excited about in school? What are the projects felt rather fulfilling to you? Think about your friends. What are the most intense memories with them? Good and bad. Who were the folks you were always on board with? Who were the folks who always rubbed you the wrong way? What do all these answers have in common? Look for the pattern. What is the ultimate north star for all those things? What's the through line?

   This requires a lot of soul searching, but trust me, this

will be infinitely helpful to you not just with dating but in life. Pointing out your values and what you believe in will help you stand out from the crowd.

Once you have the reason, write it out as "I believe in _____." Here are some examples:

- I believe in thinking differently.

- I believe in blending in.

- I believe in family.

- I believe there are better days before us then what we leave behind.

- I believe in a hard day's work.

- Mine is: "I believe in laughing at myself."

2. **Write your authentic description.** You know your *Why.* Use this format: Why. How. What.

   1. Why you do the things you do.

   2. How you do those things.

   3. What you appreciate in a date.

This root format comes from Simon Sinek as well. He calls it the "The Golden Circle."

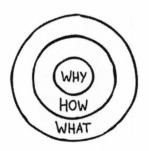

First, list your *Why*. This is the answer you discovered from the questions earlier. Second, list *How you do those things*. This is your evidence that points to your *Why*. It proves you walk the walk, so to speak. Third, write *What you appreciate in a date*. This should create an image rooted in your *Why* that your matches can see themselves in with you.

Here is my date-winning CoffeeMeetsBagel description:

I believe in laughing at myself so I can inspire others to live a stress-free life.

When I was wandering on a hike I stumbled on this old SHIPWRECK I saw last week! (It's in my photos – check it out!) I like driving for hours on end and getting lost, Star Wars, John Hughes movies, John Green books, and brainstorming fun date ideas (maybe you'll enjoy one :P). I also like singing whenever I damn please. I'm a writer, improv performer, mentor, and general goofball.

I appreciate when my date is independent and laughs at herself, takes initiative on a date. Tries a new restaurant with me. Goes for what she wants even if she fails, and upholds herself in a classy and fun fashion. I like when she wants to fill a boring day with a fun trip!

How many times did I show I was laughing at myself?

1. I was wandering on a hike (and was rewarded with a Shipwreck)
2. Driving for hours and getting lost
3. Singing whenever
4. Improv performer
5. Goofball

How many times did I allow my match to imagine us together?

1. Takes initiative on a date
2. Tries a new restaurant
3. Goes for what she wants even if she fails
4. Classy and fun fashion
5. Fill a boring day with a fun trip

Again, I'm not listing a bunch of traits I want in a girl. But how this contributes to the overall picture of us together. (I also sprinkled in my interests such as Star Wars to attract anyone who shares the same interests.)

This is how you paint an authentic picture of yourself. One that offers the truth and invites people you'll more likely click with. Everyone wins.

Feel free to combine this method with the earlier "playful" listing methods. See what works for you. You will need to be flexible with your descriptions since certain dating apps have word count limits for descriptions (Bumble allows a particularly small description.) Be constantly inviting.

Avoid This in Your Description

Let me also provide a small list of things that aren't inviting in a profile:

- **Avoid writing only one sentence** or phrase. This is not inviting. Anyone reading your profile will feel blocked off from you.

- **Don't list shallow deal breakers.** Even if you're joking.
  - Example: "If you don't watch The Office, this isn't going to work out."

  - This joke gives off a dismissive tone. Anyone who doesn't fit this highly specific category, feels unwelcome. You ruin your chances of meeting someone who could be a great match. It's a disservice to yourself because you don't actually define yourself strictly by one arbitrary sitcom. But it's also a disservice to the other person looking at your profile because now they get to miss out on who you are all because they don't watch a sitcom or drink coffee or whatever. It's a weak, arbitrary deal breaker. It's not inviting.

- **Avoid sharing your Instagram/Snapchat name.** Like I said with photos, a person can get the wrong impression of you from a photo out of context. It's best to give that info later.

Remember to be constantly inviting. A match should want to be with you in this picture that you're building. A match should want to experience your playfulness in person. Setting up your description as an invitation creates attraction and desire. This makes it easier for someone to select you as a match when the time comes.

Pep Talk #6:
Dating Apps are Like Going to the Zoo

You have a lot of advantages when meeting someone in real life first.

You have an incredible frame of reference of who this person is when you first meet.

Maybe you met them in a mutual group of friends; therefore, you know they obviously must be some what "cool" because they know your friends. They share similar values, interests, and beliefs with you and your friends. Of course, from there you have the advantage of asking your friend Sarah, what this girl or guy is actually like and can get more of a sense of who they are.

But maybe you didn't meet them through friends or through anyone mutual. Maybe you met them at work or on a college campus or at a coffee shop. And maybe you don't even go to that coffee shop a lot. Maybe it's your first time in this coffee shop. Even then you have a huge frame of reference! You're catching them in their natural habit and routine.

You know they like coffee enough to go out and get some. Most likely, this is a coffee shop they regularly attend, so they like to associate themselves with this shop (Starbucks is for business/convenience folks, or there's a snobby hipster coffee place or a cozy mom and pop shop). And you know they're here at 2:30pm as opposed to the morning, so they're a person who may relax with a cup of coffee than get morning energy from it.

Maybe they have a laptop out. Maybe they have a book they're reading. Maybe they're simply sitting with their coffee choosing to people-watch and take in the day because no one does that anymore.

Maybe they're wearing a cardigan. Or business attire. The social signals are everywhere.

Either way, without knowing it you've gathered such a frame of reference of who this person is before you've interacted with them. Before they come in contact with you. Before they're on a first date. Before they put on their best face for you, and you for them.

You've seen them in their normal state of being, untouched by your presence. That's huge.

When you meet through a dating app...

...you may chat for a moment or for days, and all you have is text that may or may not be true and a few profile photos of the person already putting on their best face.

You lose those subtle social signals.

However, you do gain *a few key insights* with dating apps.

You know this person is looking to meet someone. You know this for a fact (or else they wouldn't have the app).

You know what topics are good to bring up. Through their profile, you can figure out if you have big things in common. It's hard to go up to a stranger and randomly pick a relative topic.

That's huge! That's such a big help!

You know this person is attracted to you when you two match. You gain the knowledge (and therefore, the confidence) that this person is interested. You don't have to worry and wonder.

These dating apps help streamline the process of getting to a first date naturally. They help give a great initial push.

But you're still losing that whole frame of reference.

With an average first date from a dating app, you start at an *isolated event.*

You meet this person with no prior context.

You meet at a neutral place like a generic coffee shop, bar, or park. It was close by for both of you. It wasn't likely an extension of who you are. It's as arbitrary as sitting at a bus bench.

You talk with each other about the basics: family, job, hobbies, and dreams. But unless there's an initial spark, you still feel like that person is a stranger.

Because they *are* still a stranger.

It's like going to the zoo. You go to the monkey exhibit, and you can sit in front of the glass all day and learn about what the monkey does, how it eats, and where it likes to climb. But at the end of the day, you're still watching them in an artificial habitat and separated by glass (or the glass of your phone) and never get past a certain point.

You're still isolated.

So with dating apps, there are trade-offs. You can quickly find someone interested in you and find topics to talk about, but it may take a little bit longer to feel like you know that person well.

When meeting people through real life circumstances, you know who that person is on a basic level, but you don't know if they're interested in you, and you could have zero idea of what to talk about. It all depends on what you prefer.

Chapter 7:
The Match System

Now that you've made your profiles, you're ready to start using the apps on a daily basis to find matches and go on more dates.

When it comes to looking for a match on a dating app, it can be a crap-shoot. We all know when we personally find someone attractive, when we have shared interests, or when a person may simply be intriguing.

But there are a lot of low-quality profiles. Some profiles only show you one photo. Or a description may say less than five words such as "I like tacos." Sometimes, a person can be flat out lying on their profile, but we have no clue.

Selecting Mates

The dating app chat is where most of your potential dates

go to die. What I want to provide you is a system for liking profiles that will work in tandem with how you will talk to them in a dating app's chat later. This system will be helpful because if you end up talking to a match without the right tools, you're more likely to fail.

Be pickier than usual. Don't swipe on everyone. Seek authenticity in people's profiles. That's my quick tip. Given we all have our own tastes in the people we want to date, I am not going to give you a system about who you should like based on what criteria. Trust your instincts.

Before you like someone's profile, make sure their profile also meets these needs for chatting later on:

1. **Make sure you can find at least two things to ask.** Before you even look at photos, see how much the person has written in their description. Find info you like that you can ask them about in the chat later.
   o If you can't find two things, search through their photos. They may have a photo showing an activity or outing you can ask about.

   Pro Tip: See if they have mentioned any food/cuisine they like to eat. That can come in handy for a breakfast, lunch, or dinner date in the near future.

2. **Are their photos authentic?** This collection of photos is what they decided to show you about themselves. While they look attractive, do you feel they are portraying themselves authentically? If not, they're probably not going to be much better in-person.

Pep Talk #7: Men vs. Women with Dating Apps

Dating apps tend to work different for men than women.

Women are primarily the sexual selectors in life and so is the same on dating apps. Because of this, women will have more matches than men on average. In his book *Dataclysm*, OkCupid Co-Founder Christian Rudder pointed out, "According to data from Facebook's app Are You Interested, women, in general, see three times more interactions than men do, but Asian women were particularly successful at catching a man's interest." He shared the following graph from OkCupid's own data, too.

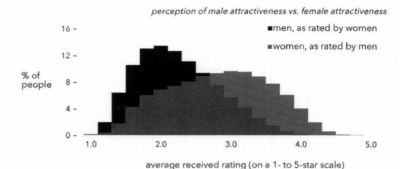

average received rating (on a 1- to 5-star scale)

Notice how even the light gray bell curve is compared to the black bell curve? As Christian Rudder illustrated, "Men are far more generous than women in matching. Here the male coin is fair, coming up heads (which I'll equate with positive) just about as often as it comes up tails. But in our data we see that the female one is weighted; it turns up heads only once every fourth flip."

Because of this dynamic, women have more freedom of choice in picking mates. This can be good or stressful. Women have more opportunities to agree to meet in person. But women also have to filter through the less than desirable matches. Some matches don't know how to chat past an awful pickup line. Some matches want to send naked photos before the time is ripe for that sort of thing. Some matches can't get their act together when scheduling a date.

If you're a woman, this can make you stressful or anxious. For example, I had a friend, Stacey, who had a good thing going with a guy in the chat. She even made the first move — she asked him to dinner for the coming week. He agreed. She told him she would like to eat Korean BBQ, Mexican, or Thai.

She said he had to pick the restaurant. Let me pause here for a moment. I thought Stacey set up the expectations wonderfully. She spared the man from rejection, and she also created a space for him to contribute some effort to the date. He had to the pick the restaurant. This is an invitation to build this relationship on teamwork. Both partners can lead in their own areas to materialize this date. This sounds small, but this is approaching a date with the attitude of serving.

So what restaurant did he pick? Answer: he didn't pick a restaurant. He didn't give her an answer. When she followed up with him a day or so later, he made excuses of how he couldn't find the right restaurant. In Los Angeles, there are plenty of these restaurants to go. But he was unable to make a small decision like picking a restaurant. This person wasn't ready for a date. He hadn't sorted himself out enough to know if this date was worth making a decision on a restaurant. Saying the date's worth was based in that decision may sound odd, but it is nonetheless true. To him, a date was worth enough for him to keep chatting to Stacey for a week, but when he was asked to contribute effort, he was suddenly unable to contribute.

I feel for women in this situation. You usually have the complex task of filtering through matches who may or may be able to materialize a date. Determining who is worth your time can be tricky.

Safety is also a primary concern for women when going on dates. Meeting a stranger can feel like a gamble with life if you're a woman. There's a reason why no one meets for a date in a dark alley…obviously. A match that proposes a date with a vague location at night in a questionable area shows little concern with their date's safety… at best but signals an early death at worst.

Therefore, women seek a target level of certainty to feel safe enough to go on a date. Women can grow frustrated with dating apps because they never feel safe enough to say yes to a date.

So being a women can be frustrating to say the least.

Men more often have the task of materializing the date from asking, to choosing the location, or scheduling the day and time. This can difficult enough, but you also risk rejection at each step. You risk your match losing interest. Women don't risk their match losing interest as often.

Men also don't receive as many matches as I stated earlier. So the risk of rejection can then have high stakes since men don't have as many chances at bat afforded to them in the first place.

The strategies in my book are designed to ensure the best outcomes for both men and women. Women will having an easier time filtering men who use the strategies in the book. (It most likely feels like a no-brainer to go on at least a first date with a person who uses this book.) Men will have an easier time materializing dates as my strategies make it less stressful for matches to make decisions with confidence and security.

Be aware of your match's needs. Serve your date, not yourself.

Chapter 8:
Chat Up Your Match

Alright, you've been selecting strong profiles, and you've started matching with a few people. We've solved Speed Bump 1. We're moving on to Speed Bump 2.

Speed Bump 2: When you do match, you can chat, but people are often hesitant to respond, so you can't start a conversation.

Now, how do you talk to a match? How can you guarantee a response? You can't get a date if nobody is talking to you.

How to Chat with Purpose and Get a Date

Chatting on a dating app is different than in-person. If you say *Hi* to a stranger in-person, social law demands a response out of sheer politeness. But on a dating app, you need to sell yourself a bit. And you're not selling yourself on your fun facts. You're not going to be judged by what you say about yourself. **You'll be judged on what you ask your date about.** You'll be judged on how much attention you're willing give them. So have genuine curiosity about your match.

The dating app chat only exists for two reasons:

1. To give your match a glimpse of you so they know you're a normal person. And vice versa.

2. To exchange numbers and set a time/place for a date.

People get so stuck on the first reason that they lose sight of the second reason. You're not here to only have conversations over phones. You want a date. Don't lose sight of this.

Here's the steps you should take when you start a chat with someone:

1. **Send a message as soon as you match** with someone, send them a message immediately. Start building momentum.
   - What you're doing is striking while you're still on their mind, while they're excited they matched with someone.
   - Send them a message even if you're no longer interested in them. This is good practice.

2. **The first message needs to include three things:** their name, mention of a fun fact from their description, and a question related to that fact. See Figure 6.

- Formula: "Hi *name*. So you have *a fun fact*. How long have you had *that fun fact*?"

- Ex: "Hi Tamie! So you lived in Germany for 2 years. What did you enjoy most about Germany?" Everyone loves to be called by name. This make you more personable than other matches.

- Mentioning their fun fact and asking them about it shows your interest in who they are, and that you want them to talk about themselves. People love talking about themselves!

Hey ▬▬ It says you know a chain of guys that leads to great tacos? Where are these great tacos?

1:01PM

Hey Lewis - they're kinda far - all the way in San Diego but they are totally worth the drive

1:40PM

But I believe that good tacos are worth driving for 🚗

2:07PM

Haha that sounds like a good trip. I have a similar philosophy to about hot dogs. I would drive to Long Beach for the best dogs I know.

4:31PM

Figure 6: a conversation I had on the dating app CoffeeMeetsBagel

3. **They will reply** if they actively use the app. Now you're off to the races.

4. **Continue asking them questions** about topics they shared in their description or in the chat.

5. **Start relating the topics back to you** after you've let them talk for a few minutes. Let them ask you questions. Just don't hog the attention.

6. **Let the conversation branch out into other directions** if it's flowing naturally. If you haven't, ask them about the two things you found interesting about their profile.

7. **Give them a reason to return to the conversation later.** Sometimes you may need to stop chatting because you need to go to bed or you're busy. But saying "talk to you later" may end the conversation because your match essentially has no reason to return other than their small curiosity about you. Instead of saying goodbye, write "I need to go. But let me leave you with one more question," Followed by a question about them.

8. **The match will answer the question.** And you can respond to their answer the next time you're free to chat. This frequently works.

Now you have a conversation going. Exciting. You've already made it farther than most. You've also solved Speed Bump 2. But you didn't come here to have conversations over phones. You want a date. Never forget this. Humans before technology. Keep building momentum.

How to Move Beyond the Chat

How do we handle Speed Bump 3?

Speed Bump 3: If you do talk with someone, setting up a first date can be hard because of the fear of rejection and schedule availability.

Let's address this problem in two parts:

1. Fear of rejection

2. How to ask for a date

How do we solve fear of rejection?

1. **Practice. Get used to rejection.** Matches will tell us "No." It is unavoidable. We have to get good at hearing "No," and choosing to move on to the next person. Instead of hearing "No," choose to hear "Next."

2. **Choose to ask someone out within the first 24 hours.** Put pressure on yourself. Decide whether you will ask a person out in this time frame. This doesn't just go for men either. Women can take control in this way as well. Stop waiting.

Most people will start a conversation and continue the conversation for days or even weeks but never have a date. There's no need for a conversation to go longer than two days with no request for a date.

Pro Tip: When you first start a conversation, play a game with yourself. It's called, "In how many messages can I seal a date?" Lowest score wins. This keeps you focused on your end game mission.

How do you ask for a date on a dating app?

Simple. Once you can confirm they're comfortable with you (usually 10 messages from them is plenty), ask something like this:

Would you like to go on a date sometime? Here's my phone # _____.

This is all you need to say. Make sure you say the word **date** and the word **sometime**.

Date: This keeps your intentions clear with your match which keeps them at ease.

Sometime: This makes it easier for your match to say *yes*. They can say *yes* without rejecting the day and time. It doesn't put your match in a corner.

This question is fantastic because what you're actually asking is "Would you like to go on a date with me ever? Is there any interest at all? Whenever you have time in your life." Given they matched with you, they likely have some interest in you.

Mind you, you should receive a *yes* or *no* answer. If you don't, your match is stringing you along.

Finally, offering your phone number shows you want to get off the dating app. It's the only actionable step forward in the relationship you can take before a first date. Offering your phone number is also a closer for the date because if your match gives their phone number in return, they are proving to you that they want the date in more than just words.

Only SMS text your match from here on out. (The point of a dating app is to find someone and get off the app, so going back to the chat can send an odd, back-pedal signal. You'll also forget where you sent certain messages.) Scheduling the date takes a little bit of back and forth, but keep the exchange as minimal as possible.

Pro tip: If you feel uneasy about meeting a match in person before you choose to agree to a date, you can ask them to do a video call for 10 minutes. This can help you make a more informed decision. If they don't agree to a video call, it may be best to not agree to a date. Also while this can save you time and money, remember that some people shine better in-person than on-camera.

Once you have setup a day, location, and time – CONGRATULATIONS! You now have a date! Plus, you solved all three major Speed Bumps with dating apps! You are now efficiently building momentum. You are starting to put a human before technology. You are serving your date. You are being inviting. And you chose to laugh at your earlier methods and try something new!

While you may feel tempted to chat more after setting up the date, there's no need. Save your conversations for the first date instead. Again, you're supposed to be talking to this person face-to-face rather than through a screen.

Don't Look at Their Social Media

Don't scan through the person's social media too much. Most of your first date is spent asking the person questions you can easily get answered through social media. There's no need to look at their photos from 2012, their "about me" section, the fan pages they like, and their last Buzzfeed quiz. *Of course, you should make sure they are who they say they are,* but over-exposure lessens your first date experience. If you already know this information, you'll have lost your natural curiosity to ask. Or worse, you'll tell your date what you already found out, and he/she will feel like there is less to tell you. Serve your date. Give them a full experience.

Pep Talk #8: Have You Fallen Victim to the False Lens of Bumble?

Bumble is a curious little app. Bumble looks like Tinder. But it has one rule that changes things a little.

On Bumble, if a boy and a girl match, the girl must send a message first to start the conversation. The girl is required to take initiative. It can feel refreshing for guys.

The main reason that girls are asked to initiate on Bumble is because a common pattern on dating apps is that trashy or desperate guys will match with a girl and immediately start asking for sex, sending unsolicited dick pics, or start making compliments on the girl's body that are certainly not a good opener.

Bumble chooses to give girls a built-in filter as a defense. Girls can match and not worry about their phones blowing up with pictures of genitalia. They solely can choose to start a chat if they think a guy will be a bit more polite or if they're willing to risk hearing another sex proposition.

It's nice that Bumble thought of this, and it gives women a more empowering feeling as they navigate the app.

But that's kind of the extent of what the filter is used for.

There's a misconception on Bumble that goes:

"Because a girl has to initiate the conversation, the girl will take more charge in the relationship. She'll try to woo a boy, and therefore, the boy doesn't have to worry about doing all the work."

This is a false perspective.

Women still want *men* on Bumble. They want a guy to take an interest in them, ask them questions, make them laugh, and make them smile. A guy still has to do all the expected wooing on Bumble like any other app.

If you men are not convinced, I'd like to ask you:

When using Bumble, how many women have asked you out on a date?

Maybe one. At best two women. And those women are most likely outliers.

At the end of the day, the guy still has to pop the question for a date, a hook up, or a meet up.

It's not that girls can't do this. They're freely open to doing so. But most women (at least in America) weren't raised to ask for a date. They were raised to expect someone to ask them. So they wait. And if they want to ask a guy out, they still may not because they're as nervous as men about rejection. They're not sure what to say, and they don't have as much practice at asking someone out as the average guy.

Don't believe me?

Nine times out of 10 when a girl initiates a conversation with you, the message she will send will be something like:

"Hey."

"Hey. How's your day?"

"Hey. What's up?"

Girls I know complain to me about guys starting conversations this way. They wish the guy took an interest or asked them a question or at least had something better to say than just, "Hi."

But girls do the same thing. Which is fine. It's funny.

Here's the real catch with Bumble:

It can be harder to woo a girl on Bumble, if you don't know what you're doing.

Since the girl initiates, it can feel like she's taking the lead in the conversation. But the guy still has to lead. And now he doesn't even get to send the first message. He'll feel obligated to respond to her first message.

I've already explained it in my conversation about how to approach the chat, but let's apply it to Bumble specifically.

When she says, "Hi. How's your day?"

Simply reply, "Hi Tracey. My day is going great. Hey, where was that photo of you in the mountains taken? It's beautiful!"

Again, say her name. Ask a question from her profile. And reply to her question.

Bumble is a great app. Just don't let it trip you up.

Chapter 9:
The System for Generating Date Ideas

You need to prep your arsenal of date ideas. If you don't have ideas handy, you will lose momentum. You will fall back into decision fatigue. You have to stop to think about where and what you will do on a date every time you have a new match. Where will you go with this person? What will you do together? People you date want to have a say, but they often expect there to be a plan.

Either you or your date needs to have plans in mind. Go ahead with a date's plan if they have one. It's best if you prepare a plan just in case. You won't slow down your momentum. You'll increase the chance of having a good time on these dates because *you* created a plan and *you* know what to expect. In fact, you'd be better off with a few plans. Plans don't require a lot of effort, and you'll increase your confidence tenfold.

Here are some of the systems for dating plans I use:

- A General List of Dating Ideas

- Weeknight Deals & Events

- Ways To Ask Someone Out

- List of Gift Ideas

Note: I explain plans and ideas for First Dates specifically in a later chapter.

A General List of Dating Ideas

This system is pretty self-explanatory. This takes about 15 minutes.

1. **Write down as many date ideas** you can think of. Going to the beach, getting coffee, hikes, going to the zoo, etc. Think of all the dates you've ever been on and what you did. Do this until you've emptied your imagination and memories.

2. **Use Google.** Search *"Best date ideas"* or *"25 cute date ideas"* and scan through the first page of articles. Add to your list the date ideas you think you'd enjoy with someone and that might make a good impression.

You should now have a list of 15-30+ date ideas. This list of date ideas has some inherent strengths and weaknesses.

The Weaknesses

Most of the ideas will be *rather generic or oddly specific*, so the novelty wears off easily. This means you'll take a person on one of those dates, but given that you need a variety, you may not be able to repeat that certain date again for a year

The Strengths

This list gives you a good mix of standard and creative date ideas that you can do any day any time, and you don't have to waste time thinking later when you need an idea for your next date.

> **Pro Tip:** If you organize this list a bit, it may be best to categorize by: Cost, seasonal, outdoor/indoor, or time length.

Here are some of my dating ideas:

1. Bowling and play "Lowest score wins" (Keeps the pressure off)
2. Go to a bookstore with a pack of post-it notes and write notes in our favorite books to future readers
3. Arcade
4. Thrift Shopping
5. Road Trip
6. Karaoke Night
7. Water Park
8. Fashion Date (Dress in a different style than you two would normally wear and meet up)
9. Sunrise & Breakfast
10. Test Drive Cars

Weeknight Deals & Events

This system asks that you create a weekly date location schedule. It's great as you can use it weekly, and it doesn't wear out too easily. Furthermore if you've recently moved to a new city, this exercise will help you become familiar with the regular local events that are affordable.

1. **Write out the days of the week** (Sunday through Saturday) on a sheet paper.

2. **Starting with Sunday, Google search: *Free Sunday Night (Your City).*** Check out sites like Yelp and Timeout and see what free or discounted events you can find.

3. **Write the down the enjoyable events for Sunday.** Write down the events, restaurants, etc. you personally think a date will like. Serve your date.

4. **Do steps 1-3 for each day of the week.** Sunday through Saturday.

5. **Your week should have variety.** Fill up each day with a fun date outing. Make sure you have at least one day in the week fulfills the following pursuits: Music, Comedy, Museum, Dinner, Movie, Miscellaneous.

   Pro Tip: Make sure every night doesn't take you to the same district of the city, but rather takes you to different neighborhoods. Variety, variety, variety. Also for the night that fulfills *Dinner*, have two or more restaurant deals listed. Your date may not want a half-off burger, but you'll have it covered when you can easily suggest $1 tacos instead.

   The Weeknight Deals & Events system has major strengths and minor weaknesses.

The Strengths

You have something in mind for each night of the week, so

even if your date plans fall through for Tuesday, you can easily reschedule for Thursday with no hiccups. If you are dating multiple people for a time, the same strength applies as you can have multiple dates during the same week with no hiccups in planning. A final strength is if you and a date enjoyed what you did on Monday night, it happens every Monday, so you can start a regular ritual. And again, all the events will be affordable or free, so you can sustain your dating life! Due to the weekly cycle, this system doesn't wear out on novelty as quickly as a list of random date ideas.

The (Only) Weakness

If you and a date only have Wednesdays free for each other, you can't rely on the same Wednesday night plan with him/her. But that will likely be a rare occurrence.

Here is an example of my Weeknight Cycle in LA for 2017:

Sunday

What: The Spare Room Roosevelt Hotel Comedy Bingo Night
When: 10:00pm–12:00pm
Cost: 1 drink

OR

What: ASSSSCAT UCB SUNSET
When: 7:00pm
Cost: Free

Monday

What: The Satellite Silver Lake Free Upcoming Bands
When: 9:00pm
Cost: Free

Tuesday

What: Regency Theatre Month Old Movies
When: All day
Cost: $1.75

Wednesday

What: Candela Taco Bar $1 Tacos
When: All day
Cost: $1 per Taco (with drink purchase)

OR

What: Park Restaurant $6 Burger Nights
When: 6:00pm
Cost: $6 Burgers

Thursday

What: MOCA Grand Ave Free Museum Admission
When: 5pm–8pm
Cost: Free

Friday

What: UCB Franklin Harold Nights
When: 6:30pm
Cost: $5

OR

What: Baby Wants Candy Sunset
When: 7:30pm
Cost: $12

Saturday

What: Royce's Arcade Warehouse
When: All Day
Cost: $3 all-play

Ways To Ask Someone Out

This system is a list of ways you can ask someone out on a date. These by no means need to be used on only first dates. In fact, you may find them better suited for later dates. Serve your date by giving them unique experiences.

Write out five to 10 ways to ask someone out that are "out of the box"

Pro Tip: It may be easier to come up with fun ways to ask someone out when you have a specific date in mind. Ex: Cafe or Bar Date – Leave a shot glass in their mailbox with a note that says "Give me a shot?"

Writing out this list is not a system you'll be leaning on a whole lot. However, a list of these asking out ideas comes in handy to switch up the boring routine of setting up a new date for the week. In my opinion, this list is more effective after you've taken a person out on two to three dates. You will have likely established a flirty rapport by that point.

The Strengths

This system allows you to show your personality, give him/her a cute memory, and separate yourself from the rest of the people he/she is used to dating.

The Weaknesses

Once you've used an idea on this list, you can't usually recycle it for later use with the same person. You should keep adding to this list periodically.

Here is my list of Ways to Ask Someone Out:

Puzzle

This idea is good for asking your date to a game night.

Have them solve a small puzzle (on the back of the completed puzzle is a note where you're asking them out).

Coffee stirrers

Get a jar and some wooden coffee stirrers.

1. Write on one stirrer (so it sticks out): "Do you like it hot or cold?"

2. On the back of the stirrer write the address, date, and time you want them to meet you.

3. Leave the jar at their place somewhere they'll find it. And then point it out to them some time later, so they notice if they don't.

   a. *Alternatives*

   b. Shot Glass - Cafe or Bar Date - "Give me a shot?"

   c. Guitar Picks - Concert - "Take your pick?"

   d. Jenga Tower - Game Night - "Would you roll the dice on me?" or "Can I slowly, carefully, ever so gently, nudge you out of the house with me tonight?"

Fortune cookie note

Ask them out to dinner, perhaps to a Chinese restaurant, by way of them opening a fortune cookie.

Improv Show (suggestion)

One of you gives each other three one-word suggestions. From there, make a date involving all three words in some way.

Script

Write a script involving you asking them out where he/she finishes the last line answering "Yes" or "No."

Calendar Date

Have your date mark a date on the calendar as "TAKEN" (he/she doesn't know what activity he/she is picking). You will go out on that date with a pre-planned outing. This idea is compatible with your Weekly Cycle System.

List of Gift Ideas

This is another system you won't be using every week. But it helps you break up the ruts of dating we often find ourselves in.

Write out five to 10 gifts you can give a person you've been dating for a little bit of time.

Pro Tip: Watch some romantic comedies and search through Reddit threads on the internet to gather ideas.

The Strengths

Gifts are a way to show a person you've been thinking about him/her. They allow you to express your feelings to him/her in a way that isn't physical or words. Plus, people simply don't give gifts to each other like they used to. It is the least common love language.

The Weaknesses

Gifts aren't something you should be giving out every date or every week. Their novelty wears off if used too much in my opinion.

Here is my List of Gift Ideas:

Mixtape (Cassette or CD)

Love note

Favorite coffee/drink

Leave roses at different places through out their routine day

Poem

Post-It notes all over their office/space

Mail a letter with 100 reasons why I love him/her

Flowers

Make a book of all our texts/emails

You are now equipped with an arsenal of ideas for dates and then some. You will not lose momentum as long as you have prepared this way before hand. You will feel like setting up dates is too easy from hear on out. Serve your date. Keep building momentum.

Pep Talk #9: American Romanticism and Mythos

Imagine it's nearing the end of high school. You've been trying to find a date for prom for months, and while you have a few weeks, you're tired of the whole thing.

It's a Friday night, and to cheer you up, your friend invited you over to his house to goof off and play some board games with his buddies.

You get to his garage and say "Hi" to everyone. You've only hung out with him and his buddies probably two times before, but you get along with them well enough to crack some good jokes.

They're still waiting on one person, but you take one of the two empty seats and start playing board games.

About 45 minutes go by when you all hear someone tap on the garage door. Your buddy hits the button and the door slowly slides up.

And there she is.

And she's not that "magazine sexy" that is always being shoved in your face.

She's pretty. In a way you haven't seen before.

The only empty seat left is right next to you. It's fate.

She sits down and suddenly the board game has stopped in favor of everyone sharing goofy stories about the last six months.

Whenever she tells a story, she looks at no one but you, so you specifically get the full experience.

Shortly, you realize you want this person around a lot more. You want her around years past prom.

This is American Romanticism.

This was a story of how I met a girl my senior year of high school. Now, American Romanticism is something I'm very fond of. I love this image. I was smitten by that girl.

After our relationship ended, I spent six months mourning everything and then spent four years trying to find that again. Not that kind of girl per se, but that feeling. Someone who fit with the image I just described.

I went out with a few girls, but never for long. Interest never increased. None of them grabbed my attention like I wanted.

I was waiting for something. Something that could come

tomorrow. Something that could come five years later. Either way I was expecting something was just going to happen with no effort from me. I would just run into someone.

I became passive. I just stopped.

Some people stay here indefinitely. They stop trying to build unique love with others and wait for someone to fit their picture of what love should be at the end.

Some people never find love because they're hooked on "the one" and reject anyone who doesn't fit that picture. Even if their dates meet 98% of the criteria. These people are not willing to go on dates and have themselves grow beautifully with another person into this new relationship they've created *together*.

I have friends who are in their 40s and 50s who can't commit to anyone because they are not interested in building a relationship with someone else. They're interested in finding love right out of the box.

In a roundabout way, they're only focused on themselves unfortunately.

It's only when you choose to take a chance with a person and choose to build something that was never there before – this is when you can find something real. Something *lasting*.

Building a relationship is about hashing out how you want to design your life with one another.

It's meeting a person and talking about how you want your relationship to be. How you two want to celebrate holidays. How you want to prevent falling into slumps. How you want your potential home to look. How you want your weekly schedule to look like.

And sure it's also you two deciding how many kids you may want and what their names should be. But also how many extracurricular activities you want your kids to be in at any one time? What values do you two want to build a family around? What kind of rules do you want to give your kids, so they grow up into great adults? How do you want to discipline them when they break a rule? How do you want to reward them when they followed a rule?

If you become married or have a long-term relationship, how do you two want to handle the unexpected problems that come up and need to be addressed? What if one of you loses their job? What if you can't have kids? What would you two do if one of your parents can't live by themselves any longer — would you take them in or put them in assisted living? What if one of your kids gets pregnant? Or disowns the family? Will you forgive them?

There are a lot of genuine plans, questions, and "what ifs" to consider as they are easily your responsibility when you have a partner for life or for the long term.

This is where American Romanticism never ventures. It never asks the questions that will need to be answered at an approaching date. It also doesn't have the answers for any of the questions I've listed. It's a picture made only for the individual and what the individual wants. It's self-centered. And when push comes to shove, American Romanticism shatters when a real problem needs to be solved.

Building a relationship on core values and getting a head

start on deciding what life you want together before you need to decide – this is a truly beautiful thing.

PART 3

HOW TO MAINTAIN DATING MOMENTUM AS YOU DATE

Chapter 10: Setting Up a First Date

When I started taking dating apps seriously, one of my first dates dumbfounded me.

I matched with a girl on OkCupid and I started talking to her. (If you're curious, according to the app we were a 97% match.)

We decided to go on a date and exchanged numbers. I recommended we go mini-golfing, and she thought that was a good idea.

What happened next threw me off.

I offered to pick her up. We lived two miles away. It was the gentlemanly thing to do. In fact, I love picking up dates at their house. It adds a lot of anticipation which is fun for me.

You start to get nervous and excited to see them. Walking

up to their door and waiting for them to answer or waiting for them to come out to your car. When a girl steps into your car, you say that cute little "Hi" to each other. Then you two are off on a little date adventure.

But immediately when I offered to pick up my date, I realized it was probably an awkward move. We had never met each other. While there was a positive experience up to that point, I didn't know her, and she didn't know me.

In traditional dating, offering to pick someone up brings a sense of security, care, and maybe chivalry.

In the dating app world, offering to pick someone up brings a sense of forwardness, domination, and feeling trapped in a corner. The same action was chivalrous in one manner, but now scary.

The dating app world has a different set of manners than traditional dating.

This may be obvious to you. So what's the point?

The girl and I still went out on our date but met up at the location separately.

I had a rocky time on our date because of this.

I didn't realize how much I depended on picking up a girl from her house. The transition from her house to the date is often filled with the small talk of "How was your day?" and "We finally get to see each other."

The drive is a natural way to warm up to each other. The girl can also observe and gather how I drive. Am I driving recklessly? Am I impulsive? Does she feel safe with me? Just the same, I can gather how she is acts. Does she nag me about when to turn? Does she demand control of the radio station? Does she trust the driver?

This stuff sounds minuscule, but all these moments to get comfortable with one another add up and can make or break an experience. If you never get into a groove with a date, you can't connect much farther than strangers.

So when we met up separately, the date ended up being rocky the whole time. I couldn't hold a long conversation with her, I was in my head a lot, and I quickly realized even though we were meeting in-person like all my other dates previously, I would need some different approaches and tools to allow me and my date to feel comfortable.

The dating app world has a different set of manners than traditional dating.

The Point of a First Date

You have a first date. Or you're planning on one. Sweet. For a moment, let's take a step back and ask a question.

We know the point of dating and the point of Phase 1, but what is the point of a first date?

You need to accomplish two things on a first date. Again, that's all. Anything else is just a bonus.

1. Learn enough about this person to determine if you want a second date.

You waste your own time if you spend an hour or so with a person and then don't know whether or not you want to go on a second date. You have done yourself and your date a disservice. You should be actively engaging with this person, not just conversationally, but also by observing how they interact with others, what values they exude, and how they respond to choices you make.

If you're completely unsure whether or not you want a second date, you need to focus on the other person more.

2. Begin setting up a second date.

If you don't quickly get a second date on the table, you will lose the momentum you've been building with this person and your dating life in general. If you lose that momentum, it can be hard getting it back because the focus on the budding relationship went away. This ultimately makes for less enjoyable dates onward as you will be trying to re-insert the lost energy and focus. When you realize you want to see this person again, don't waste much time setting up a following date. If you don't want to stop seeing this person, keep building momentum.

Location, Location, Location!

Settle where you two will have your date.

When trying to figure out the location for a first date, use this acronym. You've probably heard it before:

K.I.S.S.
This stands for *Keep It Simple Stupid.*

Don't drop $100 on concert tickets. Don't plan a five-hour outing for your first date. Don't go pick some random location you've never been to before. Keep things simple. Keep things stress-free.

There are four reasons why people meet for coffee:

1. **It's easy** (you grab a coffee then you sit)
2. **It's cheap** (on money and time)
3. **It's escapable** (they can leave at any time)
4. **It's somewhat familiar** (almost everyone has been to a Starbucks)

Make sure your first date fulfills these four reasons too.

Here are some non-coffee shop examples that fulfill the above reasons:

- Ice Cream
- Bar
- Board Game Cafe
- A Hike (on an open trail)

Keep those points in mind. If the location is not familiar to your match, I recommend the location is one of your favorite places. This way they can see you're excitement for something you like. They can start to see what makes you tick. Again, don't go nuts. There's a balance.

I recommend having a Location A and a Location B for a first date. On one hand, your date will be open to something like a coffee, but there's only so much you can learn about a person over coffee. If things are going well, and you wish to spend more time together, you can ask your date on a walk for a change of pace and scenery.

Location B needs to feel safe for your date. If you're leaving a coffee shop or ice cream parlor, your date may be weary of where you two are walking, so make sure your second location meets *all seven* of these requirements:

1. Within walking distance of Location A

2. Open space for walking

2. Well-lit if at night

3. Easy

4. Free

5. Escapable

6. Populated

   Examples:

- Park

- Beach

- Main Street in town

- College Campus

If you have these points covered for your first date, you'll be set for a stress-free date. Serve your date, not yourself. That goes double for making sure they feel safe.

Pep Talk #10: Slow and Steady Wins the Race

If dating was a race in terms of what you know about a person:

You are beginning at the starting line when you meet someone organically.

You are placed farther back before the starting line with dating apps given they provide you with minimal information.

You'll certainly feel this way. After two dates, you'll wonder why you don't feel as close with a date as you usually would if you had met organically.

I encourage you to not worry about this though.

All this means is that you'll have to go on more dates with a person. What's wrong with that? As long as you know you two click, you don't need to rush. There's still a pace.

With dating apps, you simply have a little more track to cover at the beginning.

But you can't rush trust either way you go.

Don't spill your whole life story to a person on a first date as a way to grow closer. It's intimidating to your date.

Don't rush into a make out session or sex if your only reason is "to get closer to them quicker."

You can't rush vulnerability.

Slow and steady wins the race.

Slow and steady wins the race.

Chapter 11: Going On a First Date

Nervousness can get the best of us on a first date. When I first scheduled four dates in one week, I quickly became overwhelmed. I was worried how I would be perceived. What if these women didn't like: how I dressed, how I looked, how I talked, what I talked about, how I carried myself, my stories, etc.

What if all four dates rejected me throughout the week? That'd be a huge hit to my psyche. That kind of pressure would make anybody worry. Who wants to feel that on a first date? No one. And that's exactly when I realized I was being self-centered. Those women were likely feeling anxious and nervous as well. The best action I could take was to shift the focus from my comfort and focus on *my date's* comfort instead. I decided I wanted every date to feel so comfortable with me the only question they had ask to themselves was, "Do I like this person?"

I wanted to eliminate their worries about:
Is this restaurant okay?
Why didn't he give me an address to the restaurant? Am I at the right location?
Are we running out of things to talk about?
Is this a date or is this just coffee? Or drinks?

The moment I decided I wanted my dates to feel as comfortable as possible, my nervousness disappeared. It disappeared because I was focused on what I could control – me. I could control how *I* behaved, the location we would go to, and the mood to set. I did all the prep work possible for what I could control. Our anxiety only appears when we focus on what we can't control – our date's behavior. So even if you set up a great date, your date may behave poorly. But if you did the work to provide a quality date rest assured your date was going react poorly anyways. Keep in mind, your date ideally should be focused on you the same way.

Serve your date, not yourself.

When You Leave for Your Date

Alright you know where you two are going. You exchanged phone numbers. You have agreed on a day, time, and place.

Here's some house keeping tips before you meet the person that day:

1. **Wear what your regularly wear.** Some people wonder what to wear and go all out. Laugh at yourself. Again, this is a first date. This is not a big deal. Be who you consistently are.

2. **Arrive 15 minutes early** if you wish to be prepared and

make a good impression. This also gives you breathing room if you need to find parking, traffic is bad, or something goes wrong last minute.

3. **Text your date when you have arrived at the location.** Assure them there's no rush, if they're not there yet. They're feeling the same normal tension you're feeling.

4. **Wait outside for them or grab a table** for you two if you're waiting for them.

5. **Do not be on your phone** if you're waiting for your date. Humans before technology. Just relax. Empty your mind, so you can prepare to be focused on this person for the date.

Greeting Your Date

Around this time, they may text you to let you know they're right around the corner and on their way.

How are you going to greet them for the first time?

1. **Feel free to give them a wave** if they're walking up from afar. This lets them know who they're looking for. It can be cute. Be constantly inviting.

2. **Greet them by name.** "Hi, Kayla," or "Hi, Brian." People love to hear their name. So give them their name.

3. **Give a handshake.** Simple. Firm. A handshake does two things.
   • It allows you to make touch-contact with each other very briefly. This sounds weird to mention. In America, we only touch people we have a certain level of trust with. The longer you go without

initiating touch with each other – the more awkward it can feel to initiate touch for the first time.

- A handshake offers a chance to build trust. Imagine you meet someone for the first time. You offer a handshake, and they don't shake your hand. You automatically feel more distrustful of this person. A handshake is a signal to your date that you come with no intention of harm.

4. **An alternative to a handshake is a confident hug** which can add a warm tone.
    - Walk towards them with arms open and see if they choose to come closer to you. If they do, embrace them. The hug should go no longer than three seconds.
    - You should only give this hug if you feel confident. If done unconfidently, you may seem "creepy."

5. **Lead them on to the location** once you've said hello to each other.

Should I Pay for Both of Us?

If you're grabbing coffee, ice cream, or something akin to this, you have already started wondering – should I pay for both me and my date?

Ultimately, it's up to you if you want to pay for your date. With the expectations of equality amongst men and women in America on this issue, you should feel free to only pay for yourself whether you're a man or a woman. Dating coach Matthew Hussey said it best:

"The moment you say to a person, 'You have to pay for my time,' you're saying this relationship isn't equal. 'My time is worth more than yours. So you should pay for it.' I wonder what paradigm that sets up."

Paying or not paying can also be left unsaid as you're only spending $5 on a coffee or ice cream. Don't feel like you already owe your date something. The only thing you owe your date at this point is some attention, respect, and a smile.

However, if you would like to pay for your date, I have some tips:

1. Ask your date what they would like to order. This is a classy move. When you approach the cashier, you can then order for the both of you. This shows the level of service you are already open to giving your date and the potential amount of care and effort you wish to put into a relationship. Anyone can pay for someone's order. Not everyone will choose to remember their date's order. Talk about serving your date, am I right?

2. Ask your date if they would like to find a table for you two. Do this while you wait to order. This allows your date to pick a seat that is comfortable for them. It also allows them to feel good about themselves as they now have an opportunity to serve you. Suddenly, you two are working as a team to accomplish a date even if in these small ways. The great thing is in these first moments, you are already working together.

Getting to Know Your Date

You've ordered the coffee or ice cream, and you're either sitting down or walking around. Now all you both need to do is start talking.

What do you talk about? Sure, you may have a few questions lined up. *How was your day? Did you enjoy work? Have you always lived here?* What if you run out of questions to ask?

What questions should you ask on a first date? You want to learn about your date, but you don't want to make it an interview. You want to find out what this person wants in a future, but you don't want to talk about marriage plans.

I like to follow this commonly used acronym: F.O.R.D.

1. **Family**
2. **Occupation**
3. **Recreation (Hobbies)**
4. **Dreams**

Fall back on these topics if you don't know what to ask next. It's this simple. You can start forming a good picture of a person from these questions. Plus, great conversations can branch out from these topics.

In a similar fashion, you may find it wise to stray away from this acronym: G.R.A.P.E.

1. **Guns**
2. **Religion**
3. **Abortion**
4. **Politics**
5. **Exes**

A first date is expected to be light and fluffy – a short pleasant outing – so keep it pleasant. Believe me these are all good topics that should be discussed, but not on a first date. Maybe you'll want to talk about religion if, for example, you both mentioned you are Christian or have a similar upbringing. But as a good guideline, it's not worth bringing up these topics on a first date.

Saying Goodbye

You wonder when you should conclude this first date. Even if you're having a good time, you won't want to overstay your welcome. A first date is kind of like eating a great dinner. Once you're full, eating one or two extra bites can make you think the dinner wasn't that great.

There are three ways I tend to go about concluding a date.

1. **Let your date know you have to get going after a certain time.** Do this at the start of the date. Give yourself an hour or 90 minutes – whatever feels comfortable.

   Setting this time limit expectation allows easy exiting past a certain point. Your date won't feel like you ended it too soon because you let them know ahead of time. And if you want to stay past the given time limit, you can let them know you're enjoying the date and will handle the rest of your errands another time. (This of course will make your date feel good as you are willing to make them a priority in your schedule.)

2. **The date conversation naturally dies out** past 40 minutes. Notice when your date starts having less to say. When this happens, simply wait for them to finish their thought, acknowledge their thought, then say, "Well I had a nice time talking to you. I should continue with the

rest of my day." This is a respectful way to end your date. Again, less is more on a first date.

3. **If you don't wish to see this person for another date,** you can simply say, "Well, I had a nice time talking to you, but y'know, I don't think I felt a connection. I don't want to waste either of our time, so I'll just say goodbye here." Shake their hand if you like and carry on with your day. This helps spare the person's feelings upfront rather then waiting for a follow-up later. This ending works for first, second, and third dates you're not feeling a connection with.

4. **Offer to walk your date to their car if they drove**. Do this if you did enjoy your date, and you're comfortable. It's simply a courtesy and allows for a clean exit for both of you. Once they get in their car safely, head on own your way.

However, your job is not over quite yet.

Texting Them After the Date

Once you guys have both left the date, send them this quick text:

"Please let me know you made it home safe. :)"

1. **You're sending this because you care** about the well-being of another person. Plain and simple. Make this a habit. Serve your date.

2. **You're continuing the momentum**. You'll be opening up the texting conversation in a non-awkward way again. Inevitably, your date will answer back saying something like, "I made it home." If they don't answer you by the end

of the night, you know they don't like you and are likely ghosting you, and thankfully you figured that out without wasting any time.

3. **If they do answer, reply back**. Don't waste time. Reply back something like this:
   "Good to hear you made it home, *name*. I had a great time with you today. I'd like to take you out next week. What days are you free?"

This is a quick way to put the ball in their court. Again, you'll find out right then and there if they want to keep moving forward. You're giving them a platform to tell you *Yes* or *No*.

Let's break this down:

- *Good to hear you made it home, <u>name</u>. I had a great time with you today.*

This affirms them that you had a good time with them, and you care about them. They know where you stand.

- *I'd like to take you out next week.*

This shows your date that you're willing to take an initiative. You're taking an action that matches your words. You're not just saying you like this person. You're taking steps to see this person again. You're not wishy-washy.

- *What days are you free next week?*

This is a simple question your date can answer. You don't need to overwhelm them with a list of questions like "Where? When? What time?" You're just starting the conversation by asking what day they're free. This is the <u>best</u> question to start off with for a few reasons:

1. **Your date may not know what time is best,** but they can easily find out what day they are available based on work or schedules. If they can't, they're likely stringing you along.

2. **Asking *what day* helps you prep the next date.** You can find out what is open or closed on certain days on the internet. Or you can even use your **Weeknight Deals and Events List** you made earlier on in Chapter 9.

Once they answer, you'll know where to take the conversation and hopefully begin scheduling a second date. Congratulations by the way! Because you had a first date with someone new after following these steps! You're going places! Laugh at yourself. There's more to learn!

Pep Talk #11: Dating Teaches You More Than How to Love

On one of those lovely summer evenings where the sky is clear, I went out with this girl to grab some ice cream. Let's call her Marion. Work had her running late, but she showed up with a great smile and cheerful poise.

We hugged each other hello for the first time.

"It's great to meet you," I said.

With a grin and much intentionality she said, "It's lovely to meet you, Lewis. And thank you so much for waiting."

She looked me up and down a quick moment – noting my Converse shoes, slim jeans, black v-neck, and prep school glasses.

"Well, you're quite the hipster, aren't you?" she remarked without a second thought.

Even though she threw a judgement call in the first 10 seconds, I immediately became comfortable with her.

I bought us ice cream, and we sat and talked, enjoying the evening. Around every five to 10 minutes, she kept using my name.

"Lewis, do you like your job?"

"What is your favorite color? Actually Lewis, let me guess."

"What you need to understand, Lewis, is my family plays Scrabble with the utmost intensity."

She said my name with such a cheerfulness and casualness; it made me feel good every time.

The night ended, and I was practically smitten with her. I was definitely looking forward to another date.

But I had quickly learned something that evening:

People love hearing their name in conversation.

Because I adored that Marion did this so much with such ease, I started to use it in my normal daily life as well as on dates.

I had learned to socialize better because of a single date I had on this particular evening. This was an added benefit to dating regularly unrelated to romance.

This made me excited to go on even more dates. I quickly loved noticing how others carried themselves, engaged me in conversation, as well as what they chose to not do or say.

What You Learn From Dating:

- New events and places in the city and towns nearby
- Finding out about new music artists, authors, filmmakers
- What it might have been like to grow up in Missouri, England, etc.
- New methods to stay off your phone
- How to display more confidence
- How men/women experience dating apps in-depth
- Growing more understanding of differing political views
- New apps to navigate and organize your life
- Spiritual perspectives and feelings

There are certainly more subtle benefits. But simply from going on regular dates, I grew into a better person. A person who was becoming more understanding, mature, empathetic, and familiar with neighboring towns and cities.

If anything, these things are totally worth my dating experience. They are natural occurrences of simply meeting and getting to know new people.

Dating teaches you more than how to love.

Chapter 12: Second Dates

Sweeeeeeeeeeet. We're pedaling our bike now. You had a date. You're scheduling another date. Look at you. You're in control of the pace of your dating life. You can have this second date at your own pace. You're still checking your dating apps. You're getting other potential matches. Perhaps already setting up other new first dates. This is a big moment for you.

You are fully and completely riding the bike.

You can speed it up, slow it down. You can stop it completely anytime if you'd like. But the important thing to note is you have built enough momentum at this point to just keep doing this process until you find someone you know you want to spend significant time with.

You can virtually control the pace of your dating life with no obstructions. No month-long wait times. This is what's so cool about the systems explained in this book. People of the past decades would have loved to have an option like this. People of this decade would love to have this option, and until now they didn't know they could have it.

* * *

What should be done for a successful second date?

Still follow the basic structure of the first date. Agree to a day and time, pick an event, learn about them, say goodbye to them, and text them afterwards to make sure they're home safe. But a few adjustments should be made.

The most important adjustment is:

Do not repeat what you did on the first date by appearance or setting.

I once went on a *first date* on the *third date*. Earlier I told you how I went on a first date with Marion to get ice cream and sit outside to talk. It went relatively well. For a second date, I had planned a hike for us. But given a terrible heatwave, she asked to change our hike to grabbing coffee, so we did. I like to hold my date's hand and test the mood for a first kiss on a second date. But we were sitting across from each other right up until we left. A kiss seemed less than appropriate. For a third date, I invited her to create a date, and she chose for me to visit her at her home for a witty game of Scrabble. Being invited to her home was a good sign! But we again sat across from each other at her dinner table for the whole date. We weren't even on the couch. For both of us, making a move felt forced rather than something organically occurring on the date.

All because we kept sitting at tables and talking. She

ended it after the third date.

So do not repeat what you did on the first date.

My second date rule is:

Go smaller or go bigger. That's all. This ensures the next date is different enough for you both to experience each other in new settings, moments, and conversations.

What's a smaller date look like or a bigger date after something like getting coffee?

A smaller date is intended to be more intimate. Two examples are:

- **Making dinner at your place** or theirs followed by a movie on the couch.

- **Inviting them to a picnic** in the park followed by a nice walk or nap in the shade.

Both of these ideas accomplish a few key things. First, they show off your cooking skills to your date. (If you don't already know how to cook at least one nice meal, let this be your incentive.) A person who can make a meal for you is seen as caring, compassionate, a provider, and someone who has their life together to a certain degree (in comparison to people who make themselves frozen dinners and buy fast food all week).

Inviting them to your home is a more intimate space certainly. A level of trust is needed for someone to agree. A home allows privacy for perhaps one of you to steal a kiss after dinner. A park is less intimate than your home, but more intimate than a coffee shop. If you think your date won't agree to go to your house yet, a park is a safer bet. Finding a shady tree would likely be enough seclusion to share a kiss or perhaps hold each other. A walk, nap, or movie at home is an excuse to do something while you two ease into testing the physical waters.

Simply said, a smaller date helps show the calmer side of each of you and eases you into intimacy at a smooth pace.

A bigger date is intended to woo your date with a memorable impression. Two examples are:

- **Inviting your date to a local fair** or amusement park and taking a ferris wheel ride.

- **A night date to the city** and visiting the tourist attractions all lit up.

A bigger date is for sweeping someone off their feet by doing something they do "in the movies." A date at a state fair is a picture we have seen in movies like *The Notebook* and would like to see ourselves in. Riding the ferris wheel is something we've heard other people do and heard our grandparents do – it has that old-timey, American fairy tale feeling. A night date around the city is a different picture we like to see ourselves in. Knowing that we're seeing tourist attractions that are close to home allow us to not take ourselves too seriously.

Either go for a bigger date, a showman's game — or go for a smaller date, something more intimate.

There's one more thing you should adjust for a second date. Conversation.

Share and ask for stories.

You've already talked about the surface level topics like family, work, hobbies, and dreams. Now use the topics to ask for stories.

Ask for specific stories from your date's life:

- What is your most embarrassing memory?
- How did you like high school?
- What was the best family vacation you had? Or the worst vacation?
- How did you meet your best friend?
- How did you find your current job?

Share your memories!

- What is the craziest thing that's happened to you?
- If you moved somewhere new, how was the move?
- What is your favorite childhood memory?
- Who was your favorite teacher and why?
- Did you ever pull any pranks?
- How did you prove someone wrong in your life?

By hearing stories, you're now accessing the emotional side of you. The heart stuff. These conversations help you two feel known by each other. Everyone has memories and stories to tell. Through the stories you hear from your date, you can easily learn how they react to certain situations and ideas and who they are as a person. They can learn about you. You'll start digging into the deep stuff about each other. You may even begin to trust each other.

Pro tip: Offer to share a story about you that nobody

knows. Tell your date it's a secret. This shows your date you trust them. They will find this endearing. It probably shouldn't be a traumatic story. (That's not likely endearing.) A tiny secret will do quite well. Like a time you went skinny-dipping or something cute you did for a friend that you never told anyone.

You should feel you two clicking on this date.

If you don't think you and your date are compatible, feel free to let them know by the end of the date. In a following chapter, I'll go into more detail on how to break it off with your date smoothly.

Do you want to see this person for a few months?

You should know in your gut by the end of this date. You may easily know on the first date whether you two click with each other. By the second date, you should intuitively know if this may work out or not. You have a third date to double check of course. Be honest with yourself.

Serve your date. Not yourself.

Pep Talk #12: Dating is an Infinite Game

At a talk with Google in 2017, Simon Sinek chose to talk about game theory. In this talk, he explained the difference between finite and infinite games in simple terms:

> *"Finite games are games where:*
> *The players are known.*
> *There are fixed rules.*
> *There is an agreed upon objective.*
> *Like baseball.*
> *We know all the players on the field or in the dug out.*
> *The rules for a strike or a foul ball are applied for every swing of the bat.*
> *And the agreed objective is whoever has scored the most runs after nine innings is declared the winner.*

(No one ever says, "If we just had two more innings, we could bring it back.")
Infinite games are games where:
There are players that are known and unknown.
The rules are not agreed upon.
The point of the game is to stay in the game and to out last your opponent.
Like business."

The game of dating is also an infinite game.

We never know all the players – all the people out there seeking to date.

And we have competition.

The people who can take your dates.

And the point of dating is not to win. It's not to get a date. Or to get married (another form of winning). The point of marriage is not even to win. The point of both dating and marriage is to keep dating or keep being married. The point is to stay in the game. Keep and maintain momentum.

This seems simple enough.

The issue is that we often get hung up by the people around us. Other couples who seem to be happier or more fulfilled in their relationships. Or single people who seem to have more fun and time.

So we will start to make random expectations of our relationships based on someone else's life. Assuming that someone else has it all figured out – which they don't.

Assuming that someone else is actually happier than us – which we can't possibly know. Assuming that what someone else did is even a good idea for us to do in our relationship.

The idea is to not get distracted by other people. Don't get distracted that Hannah and Chris just had a two-week vacation in Maui while you and your significant other are just working 9 to 5s.

Don't get distracted that your brother, sister, and two best friends all got engaged this year while you just started a relationship with someone.

Your goal is to stay in the game. To keep dating. Not to just get married.

Keep this in mind: Some months you're doing better than everyone around you. And some months you aren't. That's no reason alone to just stop dating or break up or get divorced. Relationships grow stronger through the harder times if anything.

With this all in mind, it's still good to observe other couples on what they do and see if it works for you tactically. But doing it just to copy them is not taking your own relationship into account. To change your relationship and your life as if you're in competition with the people around you will only frustrate you.

Keep going on dates even if you haven't found someone yet. Don't settle with someone who does not fulfill you just because you don't want to feel lonely for a few months. Don't stop dating just because everyone else seems to have it figured out (even though they don't). You're more likely to meet someone and find fulfillment if you continue to date at the pace you set for yourself.

Similarly, don't get married just because everyone else around you is getting married. Or just because your best friend is getting married. It may be the right time for your friend to get married. You may need another six months or a year. You may need to find a different person. And who is to say it is the right time for your friend to get married? Maybe they're getting married simply because one of their friends is. What a terrifying domino effect this is! So many people getting married because they feel obligated, or they're worried they'll miss out on time with their friend group. (Who is to say your friend group will last another two years anyways? Maybe somebody moves away who was the glue to the friend group. And now you're stuck in a marriage you were never really sure about.)

And don't get married just because you think it's what you're supposed to do in your 20s. Your age is arbitrary in this game. You may not be ready until you're 31. You may have been ready at 18 and still have to wait. Just go at your pace. If you're ready in your 20s, that's beautiful as well.

Your objective is to keep dating — until you find someone you want to stay with. Then your objective is to keep dating that person — until you want to marry them. Then your objective is to keep being married to them.

Dating is an infinite game.

Chapter 13:
Initiating Intimacy

Kissing is a personal and intimate thing you share with someone you care about. I take it seriously. It's not my business how you go about it or when. So I'm not going to explain how to move your lips or when to kiss – you should be able to feel that out for yourself. If you want advice on that, go look somewhere else. Google the 90-10 rule. Look up how to kiss on YouTube. Go watch the movie *Hitch*. I'm just here to guide you with the on-boarding process.

What I feel I should share with you is generally what a kiss means. I want to share what kind of step physical intimacy is for a relationship. This is based on my own experience and the moments I've observed from my friends. Is this okay with you? I'm honestly asking for your permission because if you want this advice, you can read it. If you don't, skip this chapter. Simply said, you may be looking for some clarity on intimacy. So for this moment, I want to talk to the awkward middle-schooler in your heart.

My two guidelines on intimacy:

1. Go at your own pace. Only when you are both ready.

2. Talk about expectations with intimacy early on. Ask questions. *When? How frequent?*

First of all, you don't need to share that first kiss on the first date. Or the second date. Or the third date. Or the fourth date. Or the fifth date. You can have that first kiss with your date whenever you want. Your date should respect that, no problem. I'm not even talking about asking for consent here. (That would be me telling you how to kiss.) I'm simply saying you have permission to go at your own pace. As slow or as fast as you're comfortable. Any first kiss with a new person is a special moment with anyone you date. You shouldn't have to feel like you're on a countdown with any kind of intimacy.

If you don't think you'll want to share a kiss right away, feel free to let your date know this. *Let them know where you stand.* There's no sense keeping them in the dark. They'll likely appreciate your honesty and your vulnerability in this area. You'll allow them an opportunity to be understanding.

Second, be weary of an unhealthy expectation that can start to grow. Once you share a first kiss with a date, you two will most likely share more kisses soon after. Good for you guys because I think that's lovely. However, once people start getting physical, the couple may have two different sets of expectations.

A buddy of mine explained this kind of issue to me.

He started dating his first girlfriend. They had moved from kissing to making out. After a few weeks, they made out every time they hung out. What started as five-minute sessions progressed to this obligation to make out for an hour every time they saw each other. My buddy loved his girlfriend and loved being intimate. He also wanted to spend time doing other things together. But he felt if he suggested not making out as much, his girlfriend might get the wrong idea. He was worried she'd take the request personally. All he was looking for was to make their relationship something more than hanging out and making out. But he felt he had passed the point to have a conversation about how frequent they should be intimate. He hadn't passed the point. It was never too late. But he felt pressure suggesting a change in expectations.

I bring this to your attention, so you don't fall into this rut of not speaking about expectations of intimacy. Start a conversation early about how often you would like to be intimate with one another and allow a dialogue to continue as your relationship progresses, grows, and changes.

To review:

1. Go at your own pace. Only when you are both ready.

2. Talk about expectations with intimacy early on. Ask questions. *When? How frequent?*

That's all I got for you on intimacy. This is the stuff I find particularly important in building a strong relationship.

However, if you're nervous about the first kiss, here is my only advice:

Don't take yourself too seriously. Get out of your own way.

Make a moment; let life do the rest.

Pep Talk #13:
...So One Date
Sharpens Another

Dating is a skill.

That sounds… weird, right?

Being a kind person to another person is a skill?

To be clear, there's a difference from being cordial with the general public and being intentional and attentive with a specific person.

But a lot of people don't know how to do this. In fact, most people don't have this dating skill at the start.

There are things which are appropriately appreciated after the first month of dating like making out, giving someone flowers, or a drive to the airport, that wouldn't be appropriate in the first five minutes of a date. (If on a first date, your match asked you to take them to the airport when the date was over, you'd be like… weirded out. Right?)

When building a house, there's a pace. Before the house is built, you can't move furniture in and get comfortable. There's work to be done. In the same way, you can't just move your tongue into someone's mouth. You need to lay the groundwork first. You follow?

There's a pace to building a relationship. If you and a date like each other, you'll want to keep things moving forward. But gradually. If someone cops a feel on the first date, or invites you to meet their parents on the second date, that can throw off the rhythm of what the two of you are building together. Someone who does this has not leveled up their dating skill.

Some people don't understand those big pacing steps, and a lot of us may not understand the even smaller, more nuanced pacing steps.

- The different levels of vulnerability you begin to share

- When to have that first kiss

- How to even transition to that first kiss

- How to set the tone you want for the relationship

This stuff is hard to establish especially when the dynamics change with each new relationship. We all want to get it right. But how can you get it right if you only have one date a month? How can you get in shape if you only workout one day a month?

We may need practice. We need to sharpen our dating skill. All of us. This may sound impersonal, but this practice is intensely personal.

Here's what practice sounds like:

"I want to regularly go on dates until I find someone I want to be with, so that when I do, I'll know how to treat them right. I'll know how to allow them to feel as comfortable as possible. And bring that much more joy to our time together."

This is building a skill with a purpose and a direction. This is what I hope you take away from this.

The only way you'll be able to strengthen your skill is by going on dates regularly. Once a week for example.

This skill doesn't stop at dating either. This goes all the way through marriage. Giving your significant other a surprise gift, showing them affection on a hard day or on an easy day, continuously building your trust into something as hard as stone.

You need to be continually showing affection to your significant other, and this is a skill that can best be learned before you're in a committed relationship.

As we all know, dating and wooing your significant other doesn't end at marriage.

Sharpen your skills. For your date's sake.

Chapter 14:
Third Dates

A third date is kind of like a second date.

Go big or go small again. If you went big last time, try something smaller and more intimate this time. And vice versa.

A third date can sometimes be difficult to schedule because you run out of ideas of where to go or what to do. But you have no reason to worry because you made a few lists of dates you would like to go on earlier. Use those lists to your advantage if you're blanking.

You made a list of ways to ask out your date. Now that you want a third date with this person, asking out this person in a special way from your list is something fun you can do to switch it up. It gives you a great way to kick off flirting if you haven't been flirting much up to this point, and your date will feel special and wooed by your gesture.

In my opinion, a third date should be about confirming that you're all onboard for where this relationship is heading. A third date can also establish a great sense of fun. Relationships are fun. The first two dates you two were trying to figure each other out while you did something fun in between conversations. On this third date, go full force with the fun as you have a general idea of who this person is. Now is the time to just experience them. Enjoy your date.

* * *

I decided to only cover first, second, and third dates in this book. I didn't want to go further than that for a few reasons:

- I'm only here for the on-boarding process as you decide who you want to call a boyfriend or girlfriend. I have complete confidence you are more than able to keep the momentum going past three dates. You have all the tools you need.

- Any later dates have no significant difference than what we discussed for the first three dates.

- By the end of the third date, you should certainly know if you want to see a person long term. If you are still feeling uncertain with this person by this point, there may be greater things at play, and you should move on to someone else.

Pep Talk #14:
Choose to Fail on 12 Dates

When I started dating in high school, my dad had a simple talk with me about what he expected of me and how he wanted me to treat the girls I met. Good dad, right? He also shared with me a frame of reference.

"You'll probably talk to and go out with about 12 girls before you find a girl you want to keep seeing."

This stayed with me. Before that talk, when I found a girl I liked, I put this weird pressure on myself thinking, "She HAS to be the one. I HAVE to make this work." I think most of us are familiar with this feeling.

When my dad talked to me, he essentially gave me permission to fail on 12 dates. Even more, he gave me permission to fail and still realize I was making progress.

For the average bachelor/bachelorette 20-something with

a job, seeking a relationship, I'd say they go on average one date a month.

That's about 12 dates a year. (Honestly 12 dates on average a year sounds a bit generous, doesn't it? But we'll keep it. I'm feeling generous.)

This means it will take on average a YEAR to find someone you like once you start looking. And that's the AVERAGE. It could easily take you another two to six months. Who knows really?

Either way, that's slow going. But we're used to this pace. In America, we're quite familiar with this level of productivity in dating.

We're so used to this pace that when we hear someone had three first dates in a week, we automatically assume those dates had to be impersonal. We think the guy is a douche, the girl is a slut, or the time on the date probably was completely uninteresting or filled with meaningless sex.

But at the end of the day, the person who finds more opportunity with relationships is more likely to find what fulfills them.

So change the way you think about dating. Fail fast.

Choose to fail. Don't say "we're just talking."

Choose to fail. Let the other person know you're not sure if this will work out, but you're willing to try. Just communicate this. It's endearing.

Choose to fail. When it doesn't work out, let it simply roll off. Laugh at yourself. See how much you learn.

Let yourself fail 12 times. Fail fast.

Chapter 15:
No Connection?
End It.

You will have a few dates with a person, and things will not work out.

There's no way to avoid this result. You're inevitably going to date people that you're not going to click with, and they're not going to click with you. Simple as that. It's no big deal.

I guarantee you, if you trust your gut, you will know within the first three dates whether this relationship will be worth your time. If you're still unsure after three dates, it's best to break off the relationship since not all cylinders are firing anyway.

When you need to end the connection, how do you let them know? How do you be gentle about it, but also firm in your decision? Would you do it over text? In-person?

Let's cover all this.

How to Break It Off

First of all, under no circumstances should you "ghost" your date. "Ghost" means to suddenly cut off all communication with a person with no given explanation. Ghosting is a disservice to your date as they deserve to be told. Serve your date even when it's over. Ghosting is also a **disservice** to you as you should learn how to say "no" to a person. So don't ghost.

I used to feel bad if I didn't break off the relationship in-person. For people you've dated more than two months or shared more than 10 dates with, I'd say in-person is the most respectful option.

But if you've only been on three dates with them, I'd say in-person is more disrespectful. You're going to waste their time asking them to coffee again just to tell them it's over? Especially when you could text or call? It starts to get silly.

3 Rules to Keep Your Break Up Priorities Straight:

1. Three dates or less, you only need to text.

2. Four dates and over, consider a phone call.

3. Past 10 dates, consider in-person.

Not every relationship is worth the same amount of energy. But they're worth some energy.

How to Break it Off Over Text

For texting, say something akin to this:

"Hi Joyce. I've enjoyed getting to know you these past few dates and learning about your family and your passion for animal shelters. But I can't do another date. I don't think we clicked well. Thank you for the past few weeks. You were a wonderful date."

Let's break down what this is saying.

- *Hi Joyce. I've enjoyed getting to know you these past few dates and learning about your family and your passion for animal shelters.*

Everyone always likes hearing their name. We know this. The next sentence lets them confirm you did enjoy who they were. Your date may not have a passion for animal shelters, but say something specific. Personal always trumps generic. You want them to know you are indeed being honest.

- *But I can't do another date.*

This gives you a firm stance on breaking it off. You may feel this is harsh, but people would rather they know where they stand with you instead of a wishy-washy statement.

- *I don't think we clicked well.* **OR** *I don't feel like we made a strong connection.*

This sentence helps you give a proper and valid reason for ending the relationship, but you're also not getting into the nitty gritty details. Giving someone the nitty gritty details can do more harm than healing, and it opens the door for them to prod you with questions instead of making a clean break. If you wish to be more candid, go ahead. At the end of the day, relationships end because connections are not made or maintained properly.

- *Thank you for the past few weeks. You were a wonderful date.*

The final two sentences assures the person they weren't used, it's not their fault, and the way they date was fair. Simply, a connection was not made which is neither person's fault. Again, you can go into the nitty gritty if you want, but if it's only been a few dates, it's not necessary.

Additionally, if you want to try to be friends with this person afterwards, feel free to insert this line into your message:

"I'd like keep our relationship *platonic*."

This sentence again is a firm stance. Saying "Let's just be friends" can end up being vague and a person may not feel they know quite where they stand with you in the relationship. But the word "*platonic*" is a specific word that allows a proper understanding of the absence of romance. This word settles any clarification questions.

That's the way you can approach breaking it off with a person over text.

How to Break it Off Over a Phone Call or In-Person

You've gone more than three dates. You haven't decided to be boyfriend/girlfriend yet. You should give a little more energy to breaking it off.

Use the previous text message example as a firm foundation to explain your decision to end it.

You will have to improvise since a conversation is not as clear cut as texting, but communicate clearly and go through to the end of the conversation. It really shouldn't have to be longer than five minutes. And they deserve it.

If you want to end it in-person, call them up when they're available. Ask them to meet up some place. Again, meeting up takes a bit more planning and uses both you and your date's time. This can cause you to come off like a jerk even though you're trying to be polite. But it is the right thing to do. If you're close by, it should be okay.

Make a clean break. Serve your date. Not yourself. Continue on to your next dates and adventures. Keep building momentum.

Pep Talk #15:
The Soda Shop

"Whatever happened to predictability,

the milk man,

the paper boy,

evening TV?"

Those are lyrics you may know from the sitcom *Full House*. I think we've all imagined the picturesque Soda Shop of the 1950s and wished we could enjoy it.

After all, this is how our grandparents met.

The place where everyone comes to just hang out. Buy a cute girl or boy a soda or milkshake and start talking or drop a quarter in the jukebox and a few of you begin dancing. Maybe you swap dance partners between a song because you need to move to someone new.

The soda shop was a mutual place everyone hung out, so you knew where to go when you were lonely. This was a place to meet new people and enjoy the rest of your afternoon.

Maybe you would find someone who took a liking to you, maybe you wouldn't. But you could always try again tomorrow.

And eventually you would fall in love one day. Not at first sight. Or the first week. But eventually.

I'm here to tell you this Soda Shop exists in the modern day.

It's all through dating apps. You introduce yourself to a bunch of people. You meet up and get a sense of someone. Maybe you continue seeing each other. Maybe you move on to someone new. It's mutual. We're all trying to find someone special.

The Soda Shop is not dead. It's invisible.

Chapter 16:
The Five Principles

Look at where you are now from where you started.

You've imagined a different way to navigate your dating life. You've eliminated the stress of waiting for something good to happen, and you're making it happen for you. You're learning about new people you meet and new places you visit. You've gained confidence in making your own decisions. You have plans for future dates. You know where you're going. You know when you want to end a relationship as you continue to meet others.

I'm proud of you. You've taken on the responsibility of changing the way you do things.

I want to remind you of the five principles you know well.

1. Laugh at yourself.

Don't take yourself too seriously. Be willing to make mistakes. Grow and change and try a new approach. Be malleable. Be humble.

2. Humans before technology.

You are looking to make human connections. Don't forget why you signed up for a dating app. Dating apps are designed for you to ultimately stop using them. Technology is made for humans. Not the other way around.

3. Keep building momentum.

Go on regular dates at a pace you're comfortable with. Maintain your speed. Don't stop because of a bump in the road. Keep moving until you find someone who you feel fulfilled with, and keep dating them for the rest of your life.

4. Serve your date. Not yourself.

Make life easier on them. Put others before yourself. Don't try to impress someone, but impress upon them who you authentically are.

5. Be constantly inviting.

Be open to others. Allow them to feel like they can approach you. Choose to take the risk and trust. Make it easy for people to talk with you and learn about you. Inspire others to share about themselves.

Make no mistake. These principles are simple, but they are hard to live up to. They will push you to your limits. They will help you grow. In your dating life. And in life in general. But if you fulfill all of them, your life will change for the greater good. It's not about building a better relationship. It's about building a better country.

Welcome to the SwipeLove perspective. May you continue to build relationships beyond the screens of your life.

The Brief Index & Summaries of Dating Apps

Tinder

The first popular dating app. Tinder is the most populated app. This means a bigger pool, and also means more competition for attention. Basic design, you find people one at a time by swiping left or right. Must wait for both people to like each other before a match is made. Makes finding matches take forever! There are no other major filters that help you find people you're actually looking for. Leans more towards hookups.

TLDR; A lot of people, can easily take you months to find a good match in highly populated cities.

Bumble

Same match design as Tinder. Currently has the second biggest dating pool, but significantly smaller than Tinder.

(Less competition but still good selection.) If you match, the girl must initiate the first message to open the chat. Helps girls filter through the trashy guys. Falsely gives the sense that girls will be in control of the courting while on the chat, but men are ultimately still expected to ask for the date.

TLDR; Helps girls filter through sleazy guys, easier to find a match. Men still have to woo.

OkCupid

Well-populated dating app. Makes you answer relationship questions, so you can later compare and contrast your answers with other profiles. This is useful, but not the end-all-be-all. You are free to send an initial message to anyone without matching them with making it VERY easy to get someone's attention. Allows you to sort profiles by swiping, scrolling, and seeing who's been online recently. Easily the app with the most freedom to find people quickly. Known for an active LGBTQ culture.

TLDR; Well-populated, app with currently the most freedom.

Hinge

Not super populated, could benefit from more people. The app connects you with friends of friends, figuring you will have a stronger connection from the start. Design is similar to the photo app VSCO. With profiles you scroll down through photos and blurbs about the person. Instead of liking the whole profile, you send a like of the photo and/or blurb that interested you. If the person appreciates your like, they can start a conversation and vice versa.

TLDR; Not super populated, different design. Helps start a conversation.

Facebook

Being the largest social media app, their dating feature is well-populated. Your friends don't see your dating profile, thankfully. They have a similar lay out to Hinge as you scroll up and down through photos and descriptions. They also take advantage of recommending friends of friends like Hinge and Tinder. What makes them different is they recommend events and groups based on your interests, so you have specific date outings for you and matches already at your finger tips. Your chat is text-based only, which prevents inappropriate photos.

TLDR; Well-populated, designed like Tinder and Hinge, has the strong advantage of recommending events for date outings. Text-based chat.

Coffee Meets Bagel

Relatively populated app. Not a swipe design, rather the app sends you no more than 15 profiles every 24 hours, so you're not forever swiping and can get on with your day. It's refreshing. The app also provides you with one quality profile you are likely to be interested in. To like profiles you spend "coffee beans" (an in-app currency) that causes you to only like a limited amount of profiles — making your decisions matter more. I've met great people with this app even if it didn't work out.

TLDR; The most humane dating app, great at finding a few QUALITY matches.

Inner Circle

Decently populated app with a scroll design. This app is known for its screening process to verify quality profiles and real people. After the screening, you can scroll and talk to every profile in your area immediately. You are also allowed to see who views you for free. For creating your profile, this app asks you to choose between certain dichotomies such as coffee shop/bar or early bird/night owl.

TLDR; Screening process ensures quality profiles, chat with every profile instantly.

Happn

Not super populated which works for its design. This app allows you to find people you cross paths with earlier in your day, under the assumption that it would be easy for you to meet up and have some things in common. This is best for those who live around big cities. You can essentially "poke" people and like their profile to get their attention and talk to them in the chat.

TLDR; Helps you meet people you cross paths with you throughout the day, good for city-dwellers.

Clover

Relatively populated. Seems to have a lot of bot profiles [in 2019.] Swipe design. Has an option to "Play 20 questions" with each profile you see which allows you to see what answers you have in common. Like miniature OkCupid questions.

TLDR; Tinder and OkCupid had a baby. Good, standard dating app to use.

WooPlus

Like Tinder, but for meeting plus-sized women. Not super well designed, but gets the job done if this interests you.

ChristianMingle

Relatively populated. Useful if you're interested in Christians. App is not simply designed. You can easily spend a whole day inputting your information on random topics.

TLDR; Helps you find Christians, but there are better designed apps.

Once

The design is not intuitive. Swiping feels clunky. Not populated enough. Not much else to talk about it. Popular in France.

Grindr

Hookup app for gay men. Well-populated. May be intimidating. If a straight man doesn't understand how scary it can be for women to be on dating apps, he should download this app for an hour.

Hot or Not

Like Tinder, but surprisingly not as good.

BeWild

Standard hookup app. Try it if you want another one of those.

Woo

Dating App based around specific tags. Doesn't seem too different from Tinder. Maybe try it.

Other Apps

Search "dating" in your app store and see what pops up. There are apps out there for specific needs like throuples, farmers, religions, or people with dogs. Most other app won't have enough people or just be too difficult to navigate. But always worth exploring.

Acknowledgements

I need to start with my dad, Rich, who has read too many drafts of this book to count. He has listened intently to weekly rants and tangents on the phone to parse out the message of this book and fine tune each section. This guy has been helping me write since I was four years old – and when I say "helping me write", I mean he would write my stories down for me because I couldn't spell yet. You are best example of a father I have ever seen, Dad.

I need to thank my mom, Laure, who also listened to my expansive explanations on how using dating apps effectively works – I'm fortunate she loves listening to me. I like hearing her laugh over the phone. She also took part in my early writings as a kid – designing book covers and binding them. As she is a professional wedding photographer for over 25 years, she also took the photo for my author headshot. I'm deeply grateful for you, Mom.

I love you, Mom and Dad.

Thank you to Kayla who read through the drafts and offered her often differing perspective. She has pushed this book on to many of her friends notably Sydney, Esther, and Noah, and their feedback and experiences have been gratifying. Kayla thank you for believing in my work enough to share it with the world.

My roommate A.J. has been my wingman during my experiences with dating apps. This guy joined me on double dates, listened to me rehash dates I had been on, allowed me to talk out better systems for using dating apps, and tried a few them himself even though he likes walking to the beat of his own drum. A.J. thank you for your friendship.

To my book designer, Andy Meaden, your interior design and your final cover bring a beauty and an ease of reading to this book my words cannot. Thank you for bringing your ideas to the table. Your direction for design has been invaluable to this book'. I am continually impressed by your work. Thank you, Andy! Please reach out to Andy Meaden on Reedsy.com if you're looking for a book designer – I'm so thankful I found him, and he agreed to work on my book.

To Daniel Johnson thank you for proofreading this book, I know my mistakes are many. Please seek Daniel out on Reedsy.com as well if you are in need of professional proofreading.

Thank you Kyle and Olivia for offering your photos as examples.

To the Writer's Block writing group, thank you for reading a full draft when I had first joined. While the group centered more on reading 1000 word pieces, reading such a bigger project was a lot to take on, and the feedback was the gut-punch I needed to churn out a work worthy of being a book. Being a part of your group is has been a treat for me.

Finally thank you to all those who have helped me shape this book, whether you read a draft, we had a conversation, we had a consultation, or we went on a date – I thank you for bringing SwipeLove to readers who make their relationships more fulfilling than before.

About the Author

Lewis Stone believes in laughing at himself. He believes the strength of a country is based on the strength of its relationships. He works to build stronger relationships for himself and others each day. Lewis grew up in the South Suburbs of Chicago and currently lives in Burbank, CA.

Twitter: LewisStoneSays

Instagram: LewisStoneSays

Blog: LewisStoneSays.com

Speaking Inquiries: LewisStoneSpeaks.com

References

Introduction

Bailey, B. (1988). *From Front Porches to Back Seats.* Baltimore, MD. The Johns Hopkins University Press.

Chapter 2: Why Have Dating Apps Anyway?

Adams, Scott. (2013). *How to Fail at Almost Everything and Still Win Big.* New York, NY: Portfolio.

Chapter 3: Why Do I Need Momentum?

Adams, Scott. (2013). *How to Fail at Almost Everything and Still Win Big.* New York, NY: Portfolio.

Pep Talk #5: The Yin and Yang of Technology

Le Guin, Ursula K. (2013). Lao Tzu: *Tao Te Ching: A Book about the Way and the Power of the Way.* Boulder, CO: Shambhala.

Chapter 6: The Invitation System

Sinek, Simon. (2009). *Start With Why.* New York, NY: Portfolio.

Pep Talk #7: Men Vs Women With Dating Apps

Rudder, Christian (2015). *Dataclysm: Love, Sex, Race, and Identity--What Our Online Lives Tell Us about Our Offline Selves.* New York, NY: Broadway Books.

Chapter 11: Going on a First Date

Hussey, M. [Matthew Hussey] (2016, June 4). *Who Should Pay on a Date* [Video File]. Retrieved from

Pep Talk #12: Dating is an Infinite Game

Talks at Google (2017, June 19). "The Finite and Infinite Games of Leadership[…] [Video File]. Retrieved from www.youtube.com/watch?v=_osKgFwKoDQ

Made in the USA
Las Vegas, NV
28 August 2021